D0641461

Do It Yourself

Prep N Store

Recipes & Prepping Ideas Made Easy

For more information, products and updates visit us on the web at www.prepnstore.com

Expressions of Appreciation

For my wonderful husband, Jeffrey, who never ceases to be the "wind beneath my wings." Thank you for continually blessing me and standing behind all my endeavors.

Also for my children and grandchildren who patiently "taste tested" the many recipes I've rustled up. Thank you for helping to make this book a success.

Janice Paveglio Gunther has studied nutrition for over thirty years and is a successful entrepreneur and business owner. Janice is also - and most importantly - a dedicated wife, mother, and grandmother.

Introduction

Wouldn't you love to have a fully stocked pantry with ready-mixed meals? How great would it be to have ample food available in case of any emergency? Don't you want to bless your friends and family with lovely gifts that you can make from scratch?

The information and dry-canning techniques that I share in this book will allow you to package and store homemade meals, treats, spices, grains, and much more. By purchasing ingredients in bulk and assembling your own food packages, you can stock your pantry more economically than you thought possible! With the methods I teach, you'll customize your pre-packaged meals by selecting and adjusting the ingredients to meet your dietary needs and preferences. And with convenient oxygen absorbers, your Mylar bags and jars of delicious, nutritious food will last a long, long time!

Many of my recipes require additional ingredients such as canned goods. Often, these are foods that you can conveniently keep in your pantry alongside your pre-packaged meals. I've noted these ingredients in the recipes as "Add-In." In addition to the "Add-In" I labeled recipes with "JAW" these recipes you will "Just Add Water" to prepare your prepackaged meals these will be your MRE's (Meals Ready to Eat).

I know you'll love creating, storing, eating, and sharing many great meals, treats and gifts with the help of this book!

This book has been produced by many hours of research and compiled information collected from the internet. The information that I have given in this book are only guidelines and should get you on your way in building your emergency pantry. If food is stored properly it should have a fairly long shelf life.

Be sure to read all the information in this book before starting your storage pantry and packaging the recipes.

Table Of Contents

FOOD STORAGE BASICS

RECIPES

Food Storage Basics

1
Guidelines To Getting Started

A well-stocked pantry is very important for a family to get through short-term emergencies, disasters, power outages or financial hardships. A pantry should be stocked with plenty of staples for meals, enough water for everyone in the family and foods with a long shelf life. In case of an emergency, your family would have everything it needs to sustain itself for a period of time. Begin stocking your emergency pantry by buying things that are on sale at the grocery store. Be sure to include water in your pantry.

Start by creating a plan for your emergency pantry, and build gradually from there. No single food storage plan will work for every family. This book will help you to customize a plan for your family's size, needs, and preferences.

Determine where you'll store your food. Even for a single-person household, six months of food is a lot of food, and it will consume a lot of space! A year's supply could require a whole room. Decide where you're going to start!

Your storage area should be well ventilated, clean, dark, dry, and cool. If your space is limited, be creative! Most homes have "hidden areas" that will work for storage.

Do NOT place your food storage containers directly on or against cement or earthen floors and walls. A plywood barrier will provide ventilation and protect against moisture.

Keep your stored food away from products that may affect its flavor (for example, cleaning products and chemicals).

To build your supply easily and affordably, purchase a few items each week. By using the basic foods in your daily menus, you can reduce your food costs, which allows you to purchase more supplies. Your family may decide to forego a few nonessential expenditures until you accumulate a satisfactory supply.

Label each package with the current date as you purchase or package them (for example, "10/2013"). Use the "First In-First Out" system by storing new packages at the back of the shelves and moving older packages toward the front. Use these types of food items regularly to keep the rotation current, replacing supplies as you use them.

You can conveniently supplement your pantry with store-bought dry prepackaged food products also. Just remove the food from the original packaging and repackage it in a Mylar bag with an oxygen absorber. It will keep beyond the manufacturer's expiration date.

Consider repackaging dry food products such as pasta, instant pudding mixes, powdered drinks, tea, coffee, boxed dinner mixes, dried soups, and much more.

When repackaging boxed dinners like Hamburger Helper or macaroni and cheese, cut a very small slit in the powdered sauce packet so the oxygen can be absorbed from it as well. Just place the packet upright into a Mylar bag and pour the remaining product around it so that the packet can't tip and spill.

You can add nonfat powdered milk to boxed mixes that normally require liquid milk, such as instant pudding. Just empty the mix into a Mylar bag along with the appropriate amount of milk powder, and seal with an oxygen absorber. Label your package with instructions to add water instead of milk.

Most store-bought canned goods will last well beyond the

manufacturer's two- to three-year expiration date. Don't assume it has spoiled just because the date has passed.

2
Factors In Food Storage

Temperature   The temperature at which food is stored greatly affects its shelf life no matter how well the food is packaged. If you must store your food in a warm environment, be aware that its shelf life will be significantly shorter. You should ideally find a place where the temperature remains stable at 70°F or lower. As a general rule, properly packaged foods will last 30 years stored at 50°F, 20 years at 60°F, 10 years at 70°F , 5 years at 80°F , 2.5 years at 90°F , and only 1.25 years at 100°F. (These rules do not apply to all foods.) Frequent temperature changes will also shorten storage life.

The average temperature in a residential basement is 60°F, making it an excellent location for most food storage purposes. If your home has a nice, dry root cellar, that will also work well. Many basements and cellars have concrete floors and masonry walls. These surfaces emit moisture and odor which can leach into your food over the years. Be careful to prevent your stored packages from touching these surfaces directly.

Of course, some homes don't have a basement or root cellar. In these cases, you should store your food in a dark closet or room in your home, or in the garage if the temperature is stable. If you don't have a cool location, then rotate your stored food frequently enough to prevent spoilage. The cooler, drier, and darker the environment, the better.

Atmosphere   Oxygen oxidizes many of the compounds in food. Bacteria, one of several agents that cause spoilage, also needs oxygen to grow. To lengthen your food's shelf life, be sure that your containers have an airtight seal.

Oxygen comprises approximately 20% of air. Oxygen absorber packets work by binding the oxygen to the remaining 80% of the air. Because of this, your properly vacuum-sealed bags may not appear completely airtight. Some foods will look more shrink-wrapped than others. For example, a vacuum-sealed bag of rice and beans will take on the textured shape of its contents, but a vacuum-sealed bag of sugar won't seem as tight. This is perfectly normal.

Product moisture content   For the best long-term storage, grains should have a moisture content of 10% or less. Dried foods with less than 10% moisture are very brittle and will snap easily. Commercially dried foods are well within these levels, but home-dehydrated foods usually aren't this dry and will have a shorter shelf life.

Food containers   The best food storage containers are canning jars, Mylar bags, and food-grade plastic buckets. If your plastic containers are not rated "food grade," be sure to line them with a Mylar bag. For the highest level of safety, I recommend that you store your food in Mylar bags with oxygen absorbers, vacuum-seal the bags, and then store the bags in food-grade buckets. Packages with an air tight seal will have the longest shelf life.

Dehydrated products   Many light-colored dehydrated products, such as powdered dairy products and dehydrated potatoes, will gradually brown over time. If the food has been properly stored, the discoloration does not necessarily indicate spoilage.

Risk factors   Do NOT take chances with stored foods. Throw away any bulging cans, bottles that appear poorly sealed, or foods that smell rancid. It's a good idea to boil canned vegetables for ten minutes before consuming.

3
Avoiding Food Storage Problems

Variety & Balance   As you're building your stored-food supply, don't underestimate the importance of variety! Ninety-five percent of people only store four basic items: wheat, milk, honey, and salt. That is *not* enough! It's hard to survive on such a diet for several reasons. First, many people are allergic to wheat and don't even realize it until they're eating it meal after meal. Also, children can only tolerate small amounts of wheat, so it's an especially poor staple for them. Then there's "appetite fatigue." This simply means that we get tired of eating the same foods over and over. After a few days, you'd rather go hungry than take another bite of that old repeated meal. Young children and senior citizens are particularly susceptible to appetite fatigue. As a rule of thumb, you should store less wheat than is generally suggested, and put the difference into a variety of other grains instead, focusing on the ones your family enjoys. I also recommend that you store a variety of beans to add a beautiful range of color, texture, and flavor. Remember to include other highly-flavored items such as tomato bouillon, cheese, garlic, onion, and spices to make your pre-packaged meals delightfully savory! You should keep a good food storage cookbook (along with this book) and store the ingredients that you'll use in the recipes. Don't forget: Variety is essential to a successful storage program. To keep a well-balanced food supply, buy several items rather than a large quantity of one item.

Extended Staples   It is absolutely critical to store much more than the four basic food items (wheat, milk, honey, and salt). You need a good stock of dehydrated and/or freeze-dried foods. You should also have plenty of canned goods, whether you can them yourself or buy them at the grocery store - or both. Make sure to include cooking oil, shortening, baking powder, soda, yeast, and powdered eggs in your pantry. You'll need these items in most basic recipes. In order to help you build a well-balanced pantry, I've included a list of critical food items in this book.

Quick & Easy When you're overstressed or you've been out of the house all day and you just can't prepare your basic meals, the quick & easy meal recipes prepared ahead of time are extremely helpful. Because they require little preparation. No-cook foods such as freeze-dried items and MRE's (Meals Ready to Eat) are good to have on hand also. Many preparedness outlets carry freeze-dried foods, canned goods, and MRE's.

Comfort Foods Treats like candy, pudding, and jello may sound trivial, but they can be a real solace during hard times, especially for children. Be sure to keep several special comfort foods for your family.

Containers Keep a good supply of Mylar bags and sturdy buckets. You should always store your bulk foods in sealed Mylar bags, and then put the bags into the buckets for stability. Don't make the mistake of leaving your food in paper or fabric sacks. The sacks are susceptible to moisture, insects, and rodents. Not only will you have to throw the food away, but you could wind up with a major pest problem. Also, you should never store your bulk foods in trash can liners. Even though they're "clean" out of the box, they've been treated with harmful pesticides, and you don't want those chemicals contaminating your food supply.

Use Your Storage Get familiar with the foods you're storing - now! You need to be comfortable preparing these foods. It's *not* something you want to learn under pressure. Also, let your family enjoy these foods now. That way, much of what you're storing will be perfectly normal to them. Changing your diet during stressful times can be both psychologically and physiologically difficult. You have a great food storage recipe book right here in your hands. Learn to use these foods!

Now that you know the basic food storage problems, you can easily avoid them!

4
Critical Foods To Store

Vegetable oil

Honey, sugar, syrups

Coffee

Salt, pepper, garlic

Beans

Powdered cheese

Grains, oats, rice

Dried vegetables

Dried fruits

Canned fish

Canned vegetables

Canned beans

Canned tomatoes

Chicken stock

Canned soups and stews

*Baking soda

Vitamins and supplements

Milk (dried and canned)

Vinegar (white and apple)

Bouillon flavor

**Tea

Pasta

Potatoes, instant

Dried onions

Freeze dried meats

Yeast

Seasonings and herbs

Flour

Hot cocoa

Soy sauce

Baking supplies

Nuts

Popcorn

Peanut butter

Chewing gum and candy

Pet food

Baby food and formula

*You can use baking soda as an antacid, for brushing your teeth and to fight an allergy attack. In case of a severe allergy attack baking soda may save a life. In the case of an allergy attack mix some baking soda with water and have the person drink it if they are able. This will cut the severity of the attack.

**Many teas are useful for medicinal purposes such as calming agents, sleep aids, cold and flu relief, etc. Teas can be store in a Mylar bag with an oxygen absorber and sealed for long term storage.

5
Storing The Basics In Bulk

Grains include wheat, flour, oats, corn, cornmeal, barley, and rice. Pastas such as macaroni and spaghetti are also considered grains. Make sure you store a wide variety of grains so you can suit your family members' individual needs and rotate the supply. You also need options for those who may be sensitive to a particular grain.

You have several storage options for grains. Most grains can be kept in small containers. This makes them convenient to use and reduces the possibility of spoilage. You can also store grains in heavy, tightly sealed plastic containers. I like to store grains in Mylar bags with an oxygen absorber and then put the bags in a sturdy bucket for safety.

The storage rules are very different for brown rice and for white rice. Under average conditions, brown rice will keep for only six months because the outer shell contains essential fatty acids which go rancid as they oxidize. You can refrigerate brown rice to store it for longer periods. In the absence of oxygen, refrigerated brown rice will last one to two years. Store brown rice at the lowest temperature possible. Its shelf life doubles when you lower the temperature another ten degrees. With white rice, the fatty outer shell is removed, so it's less nutritious but keeps much longer. Hermetically sealed in the absence of oxygen, white rice has a storage life of eight to ten years at a stable temperature of 70°F. It will keep even longer at cooler temperatures.

Legumes include beans (soy, pinto, white, kidney, lima, winged, red, navy, pink), black-eyed peas, split peas, lentils, and peanuts. You can easily store these nutritious, high-fiber, high-protein foods in dry plastic containers with tight-fitting lids, in Mylar bags with oxygen absorber packets, or in bulk-sized five- or six-gallon buckets.

Seeds can be stored at room temperature in a container with air, or you can put them in the freezer. They'll keep for about four years at a stable temperature of 70°F. If you want to sprout your seeds, do NOT put them in an oxygen-free environment. Seeds require air to stay viable. Pack them well, but make sure they have some oxygen.

Nuts are high in fat and must be stored properly to avoid rancidity which can cause illness. Nuts stored in the refrigerator are good for about four months. If you put them in the freezer, they'll last about eight months to a year. Generally speaking, unsalted nuts last longer than salted nuts, whole nuts last longer than chopped nuts, and nuts in the shell last longer than nuts out of the shell. Store nuts in an airtight, moisture-proof container. You may want to invest in a FoodSaver with a Mason jar attachment. This is a fabulous tool that removes the air from your storage containers.

Fats and oils are essential to every diet and are required items in your food storage plan. You should store some versatile fats such as shortening, cooking oil, margarine, and mayonnaise. Olive oil and coconut oil are especially healthy oils to have on hand. Keep your fats and oils in sealed containers in a cool, dry, dark place, and rotate them frequently.

Yeast is a living organism and therefore has a relatively short storage life at room temperature. If you keep yeast tightly sealed in its original metal foil storage containers, it should last two years at 70°F. If you refrigerate yeast, it will be good for five years. Frozen yeast will keep indefinitely.

Iodized salt, when available, is preferable to plain salt for storage. You can store salt in a cool, dry place in its original container, in sealed Mylar bags, or in tightly sealed food-grade buckets. No oxygen absorber packet is necessary.

White sugar is easy to store, and you have several good options. You can pour white sugar into a five-gallon plastic bucket lined with a Mylar bag, toss in some oxygen absorbers, seal the bag, and tightly cover with the bucket lid. If you prefer smaller packages, you can seal the sugar in gallon- or quart-size Mylar bags with oxygen absorbers and keep the bags in a sturdy bucket to prevent them from tearing. If you don't want to use oxygen absorbers, you can use a vacuum sealer to seal smaller bags (approximately 3-4 lbs. each). It's still a good idea to store the smaller bags in a plastic bucket with a lid. As long as white sugar is kept cool and dry, it will keep indefinitely.

Powdered sugar stores as easily as granulated white sugar. It won't clump because it has a lower moisture content than granulated sugar. Follow the rules for white sugar (above). Most importantly, keep your powdered sugar dry and airtight. You can use five- to six-gallon buckets, or if you prefer, use smaller Mylar bags, and then put the bags into a sturdy bucket to keep them safe.

Brown sugar has a high moisture content and may harden into a solid block in long term storage. Don't worry if this happens to your brown sugar. It's still good. You'll just need to soften it.

Here are a few simple methods to soften brown sugar:

- Place the brown sugar in an airtight container with a slice of fresh bread on top. Seal the container and let it sit overnight. If the sugar isn't soft and fresh by morning, let it sit with the bread another day or two.

- Sprinkle the brown sugar with a few drops of water, seal it in a plastic bag, and let sit for a day or two.

- Place the brown sugar in an open container and lay a wet cloth or paper towel over the container. Let it sit overnight.

- In an airtight container, lay a sheet of aluminum foil on top of the sugar, and then set a dampened paper towel (not dripping wet) on top of the foil. Seal and let sit overnight or a few days as needed. Remove the foil and paper towel once the towel is dry and the sugar is soft.

Although softening brown sugar is simple, you may choose to avoid the issue altogether by making your own brown sugar as needed. Store-bought brown sugar is simply white granulated sugar with added molasses. The amount of molasses determines whether it's sold as light brown or dark brown sugar. So, to make your own brown sugar, just mix some molasses into your granulated sugar to taste. It's that easy!

Honey is natural, healthy, and will keep indefinitely if stored free of moisture. Be wary of honey with additives such as water and sugar. The additives are completely unnecessary and deplete the natural qualities of pure honey. Additives may prevent honey from crystalizing over time, but crystallization is harmless and, in some cases, preferred because the thicker consistency can be easier to spoon and spread. If you prefer to liquefy your crystalized honey, just set the container into hot water for a few minutes. For long-term storage, keep your pure honey in a well-sealed container. Over time, it may darken. The darker honey is still perfectly good and also deliciously intensified in flavor.

Instant nonfat powdered milk will last at least twenty years if properly stored. Store your instant milk in a Mylar bag with oxygen absorber packets. Do NOT use a vacuum seal for loose powdered milk. The vacuum's suction will draw the powder into the seam, and the seal will not be airtight. Air will gradually enter the bag, and your instant milk will deteriorate more rapidly.

To safely vacuum seal your powdered milk, purchase the milk in a box that contains several one-quart paper packs, and seal one or more unopened paper packs into your vacuum bags. Simply select a vacuum bag that is slightly larger than the paper packs, or cut an appropriately-sized bag from a roll of vacuum seal material. Using scissors, make a tiny (1/4 inch) cut in the edge of each paper pack to break the seal. Place the milk packs in the vacuum bag, and seal. The air inside the paper milk packs will be withdrawn, but very little milk powder will escape. Then store your sealed instant milk inside a covered sturdy bucket in a cool, dark, dry place.

6
Food Storage Containers

The three basic containers for long-term food storage are glass canning jars, Mylar bags, and five- to six-gallon buckets. Each type of container has its unique qualities and purposes. I use all three in my pantry.

Storing with glass canning jars   Canning jars are ideal for storing homemade mixes and other foods in your kitchen pantry. They are comparatively pricey, but the glass jars themselves can be reused indefinitely. You must replace the lids for each use. I purchase canning jars when they're on sale at the grocery store, but you can also find great deals at garage sales and online.

Glass jars will keep your food safe from pests. They fit easily on small shelves, and their contents can be readily labeled and identified. The smaller quantities are also convenient to use and rotate. However, glass jars are much heavier than bags, and they can be difficult to safely pack and transport in case you must leave your home in an emergency.

Always wash and thoroughly dry glass jars before use. The dishwasher is ideal for the jars themselves, but don't put the lids in the dishwasher.

An inexpensive canning funnel is extremely helpful for pouring ingredients into jars. For layered ingredients, pack down each layer to be sure everything will fit. After filling the jar with dry food, place an oxygen absorber packet on top of the food, and then seal the jar with the lid. For increased safety, I recommend doubling the number of oxygen absorber packets or using a FoodSaver machine with a jar attachment. The FoodSaver will remove the air from the jar for a tight seal with or without oxygen absorbers.

When sealed properly, your food will have the longest shelf life possible.

Label the jar with the contents or recipe name, any preparation instructions, and the date.

Jars for gift making   The recipes in this book make beautiful and welcomed gifts when stored and dressed up in a glass canning jar! Pop a pretty bow on top of the jar, or tie a little ribbon around a small piece of patterned cloth draped over the lid. For an even bigger bang, you can tie on a new spatula, wooden spoon, oven mitt, or any other small item related to the gift. Craft a lovely tag from paper, or decorate an adhesive label with the recipient's name. Be creative with your own fabulous ideas and recipe customizations!

Using Mylar bags   Mylar bags are less expensive than glass jars. When properly sealed, the bags are adequate to protect your food from insects. However, they're much less sturdy than jars and buckets and can be punctured easily. Rodents can chew through Mylar bags. Because of their relative vulnerability, you should store the filled and sealed bags in five- to six-gallon buckets or some other sturdy, tightly-lidded container such as a plastic tote or metal trash can.

Based on your family's needs, you may want to use Mylar bags to store convenient single-serving packets of foods like instant oatmeal and dip mixes. Larger bags can be cut to small sizes and sealed around the edges with a clothing iron or flat iron for hair. Mylar bags are light and easy to transport if you need to leave your home in an emergency, and they're also a good option for shipping food gifts through the mail.

Using Buckets   Use five- to six-gallon buckets for long-term bulk storage of grains, beans, sugar, dried powdered milk, etc. Large buckets are also perfect for storing and protecting your smaller prepackaged Mylar bags.

Because buckets aren't generally a good oxygen barrier by themselves, follow these recommendations to maximize your food's shelf life: When storing bulk quantities, line the buckets with a large Mylar bag, pour in the food, and then add a few oxygen absorber packets to the bag. Push out as much air from the bag as possible, and seal. When using the bucket to store multiple small bags, you can omit the larger lining. Be sure to cover your buckets tightly with a lid. Always label and date the buckets so you can identify their contents at a glance and conveniently rotate them on a "first in-first out" basis.

Buckets are durable and stackable. A Mylar bag lining with oxygen absorbers will not only keep the food airtight, but it will also act as a second barrier against oxygen and other gasses that can pass through the pores in the plastic buckets over time. You can inexpensively purchase food-grade buckets and lids online or at a major home improvement store.

7
Sizing And Sealing Mylar Bags

Mylar bags are available in several different sizes. I use quart, gallon, and five-gallon bags. Follow the guidelines below to cut larger bags to the needed size and seal them safely.

You can purchase Mylar bags online or from a cannery.

Use a ruler and pen to draw a line down the middle, or fold in half and make a crease.

Cut along the line or crease.

Cut to the appropriate size.

(continued next page)

Iron the cut side on high to seal. It seals better with a cloth under the bag during sealing.

Use a canning funnel to pour your dry ingredients into the bag.

Place an oxygen absorber packet inside the bag.

Prepare the iron and the edge to be sealed.

Press out as much air as possible, and iron on high heat along the open edge on a hard surface to seal.

Finished package!

8

Oxygen Absorbers

Benefits of using oxygen absorbers When storing dry foods, include oxygen absorbers in your packages. The oxygen absorbers will:

- Extend the shelf life of your food
- Prevent bacteria and fungi growth
- Eliminate the need for added preservatives
- Prevent food discoloration
- Prevent rancidity
- Retain the fresh-roasted flavor of coffee and nuts
- Prevent oxidation in spices and seasonings
- Prevent oxidation of important vitamins
- Prevent infestation of bugs

Typical uses for oxygen absorbers Oxygen absorbers should be used for long-term storage of all sorts of dry foods such as:

- Hard candy and confections
- Tea (loose or bags)
- Pasta and noodles
- Dried fruits and vegetables
- Spices and seasonings
- Flour and grains
- Beans and legumes
- Powdered milk and powdered eggs
- Pharmaceuticals and vitamins

Storage of oxygen absorbers Don't open a package of oxygen absorbers until you're ready to use them. Remove only the number of absorbers you need immediately within twenty minutes of opening to retain their ability to absorb oxygen. Reseal the unused packets in an airtight container right away.

Oxygen absorbers vs. desiccants   Desiccants are for use where moisture (not oxygen) is a problem. Do NOT use desiccants for dry food storage. Use oxygen absorbers.

How to use oxygen absorbers   After filling a Mylar bag with your dry food, place an oxygen absorber packet inside the bag. Lay the bag flat or squeeze out as much air as possible, and seal. The oxygen absorbers will remove the oxygen, but because air is only 20% oxygen, the bags may appear to contain air. It's completely normal for some bags to have a more tightly vacuum-sealed look than others. Store your Mylar bags in a large, sealed, sturdy container to protect them from rodents, pests, and breakage.

Appropriate size of oxygen absorbers   Follow these guidelines to determine the appropriately sized oxygen absorbers for your packages:

For All Typical Dry Food Items*

1 quart (8x8 inch bag)	#10 can/1gallon (10x16 inch bag)	5- to 6-gallon bucket (20x30 inch bag)
100 CC	300 CC	2000 - 3000 CC

For bags smaller than one quart, you can use 50 CC. I purchase 300 CC and 2000 CC packets and use them for all of my storing.

*The chart above assumes that you have forced most of the air from the Mylar bag. If you do not remove excess air from the bag, then use a higher CC rating than recommended above.

Note on diatomaceous earth   My research indicates that diatomaceous earth is not a sufficient solution for long-term food storage. It is not used by the top professional packaging houses. In my experience, the best way to keep your dry foods fresh and safe is with Mylar bags, oxygen absorbers, and a strong, tightly-lidded container.

9
Estimated Storage Life

Unless otherwise noted, the shelf life for each item listed assumes that the food is stored in the absence of oxygen (in Mylar bags with an oxygen absorber or vacuum-sealed in a food-grade bag) and in a stable temperature of 70°F. Keep in mind that lower temperatures will increase shelf life. Studies have shown that the shelf life of many products can be doubled simply by lowering the storage temperature by 10°F. You can dramatically increase the shelf life of yeast, brown rice, and garden seeds by storing them in the freezer.

Many light-colored dehydrated products such as powdered milk and potatoes will gradually brown over time. This does not necessarily mean they have spoiled if they've been properly stored.

Don't place your food packages in direct contact with concrete flooring or masonry walls. These surfaces emit high levels of moisture and odor which, over the years, can permeate the packaging and be absorbed by the food.

Baking powder....................18 months (unopened)
Baking soda.......................... …..…8-20+ years
Beans and legumes, dried...…….................20+ years
Butter powder……................................…..5 years
Cheese, dehydrated…............................…...5-8 years
Cheese, Parmesan or Romano….10 months (unopened)
Cheese powder……...............…..................…..15 years
Cocoa powder……....................................…15 years
Drink mix, fruit, powdered........................…..10+ years
Eggs, dehydrated or freeze-dried, powdered……..5-8 years
Eggs, fresh……………….......... 120 days (refrigerated)
Flax seed……...…10 years
Flour, white, enriched…........................…12 months
Flour, white……...…..5 years

Flour, all purpose…………………………….…...15 years
Flour, bakers………………………………….....15 years
Flour, whole wheat…………………………...up to 5 years
Fruit, apple slices, dried……………………….8 years
Fruit, dehydrated…………………………………..5 years
Garden seeds without oxygen-free container………4 years
Grain, barley………………………………......8-12 years
Grain, buckwheat (a hard grain)……………….8-12+ years
Grain, corn, whole, dry (a hard grain)………..10-12+ years
Grain, flax (a hard grain)…………………….10-12+ years
Grain, kamut (a hard grain)…………………..10-12+ years
Grain, lentils………………………………....10-12+ years
Grain, millet (a hard grain)…………………..10-12+ years
Grain, oat groats (a soft grain)……………….…8 years
Grain, oats……………………………….....10-12+ years
Grain, oats, rolled (a soft grain)………………...30 years
Grain, quinoa, whole (a soft grain)………………...8 years
Grain, rice, brown……………………………….1-2 years
Grain, rice, white…………………………….8-10 years
Grain, spelt (a hard grain)……………………....10-12+ years
Grain, triticale (a hard grain)………………….5-12+ years
Grain, whole wheat (a hard grain)……………..12+ years
Honey………………………………………....indefinitely
Milk, nonfat dry…………………………………..20 years
Mixes, biscuit……………………………………5+ years
Mixes, bread mix, white………………………….5+ years
Mixes, pancake, buttermilk………………………5+ years
Onions, dehydrated…………………………….8-12 years
Pasta…………………………………………..15-20 years
Popcorn……………………………………………8+ years
Potatoes, instant…………………………….20-30 years
Pudding mix, chocolate or vanilla…………………..5 years
Rye (a soft grain)………………………………...5-8 years
Salt…………………………………………….indefinitely
Shortening, Crisco……...indefinitely (in original container)
Soup base, Tone…………………………………….10 years
Spices………………………………………….indefinitely

Sugar, granulated......................................20+ years
Sugar, brown......................................4-18 months
Vinegar, opened....................................12 months
Vinegar, unopened..............................24+ months
Yeast................24 months (or marked expiration date)
Yeast, refrigerated.....................................5 years

Note on canned goods: Most store-bought canned goods will keep longer than the marked expiration date. Canned fish is a very good source of protein and omega 3 fatty acid, and it will last many years. Hormel canned products will last indefinitely in their original containers.

Do not take chances with stored foods. Throw away any bulging cans, poorly sealed bottles, or foods that smell rancid.

10
Water Storage and Purification

An emergency water supply   We often take water for granted, but when our supply is cut off, we quickly realize that we have a health emergency. Not only do we need safe drinking water, but we also need water for basic cooking, washing, and cleaning, and even for flushing toilets. Natural disasters can interrupt the supply of water for days or weeks. Every home should have an adequate emergency water supply. Don't count on buying bottled water at the time of need. Stores sell out quickly in emergency situations.

How much water to store   Water is absolutely essential, and you should prioritize it in your storage plan. Every person's water needs are different depending on age, physical condition, activity level, diet, and climate. As a general rule, you should store at least one gallon of water per person, per day. This is minimally sufficient for drinking, food preparation, and hygiene. And don't forget your furry friends! Allow about one quart per day for each cat or dog, more for large dogs. I recommend that you keep a three-day supply at the very least, and up to a two-week supply if space allows.

Appropriate containers for water storage   You can safely store water in clear, food-grade plastic containers like soft drink bottles, or fiberglass or enamel-lined metal containers. Don't repurpose plastic milk bottles for your water storage. The protein and fat residues from milk are difficult to remove completely, allowing bacteria to grow during storage. Of course, you should never use a container that previously held toxic substances.

Before you fill your containers with water, disinfect them by rinsing with a diluted chlorine bleach solution (one part bleach to ten parts water). Replace your stored water every six months.

Treating water before storing   If your water is treated commercially by a water utility, you can store it as-is. If you're storing well water or untreated public water, you must disinfect the water to prevent the growth of harmful bacteria or pathogens.

Start with safe drinking water, and use liquid household chlorine bleach with 5.25% sodium hypochlorite. Do NOT use bleach with added soap or fragrance. Use a clean medicine dropper to add bleach to the water according to the guidelines below:

- 4 drops bleach per quart or liter of water
- 8 drops bleach per 2 quarts, 2 liters, or half gallon of water
- 16 drops bleach per gallon or 4 liters of water

When treating larger quantities of water, follow these conversions from drops to standard measuring units:

- 1/8 teaspoon = 8 drops
- 1/4 teaspoon = 16 drops
- 1/2 teaspoon = 32 drops
- 1 teaspoon = 64 drops
- 1 Tablespoon = 192 drops
- 1/8 cup = 2 Tablespoons = 384 drops

Stir the water and let stand for 30 minutes. If the water does not taste and smell of chlorine after 30 minutes, add another 8 drops and let stand another 15 minutes. Seal the containers, and label with contents and date of preparation.

Where and how long to store water   Store your water containers in a cool, dry place away from direct sunlight and away from any toxic substances like gasoline, kerosene, pesticides, etc.   Plan to rotate and replace your home-bottled water every six months. Commercially bottled water is usually marked with an expiration date. If no expiration date is given, bottled water with an IBWA or NSF seal should have a shelf-life of approximately one year.

If your water has been stored for a while and tastes stale, pour it back and forth from one clean container to another several times. This will re-oxygenate the water and freshen its flavor.

Managing a water shortage   If an emergency catches you without enough clean water, never ration your family's drinking water. Drink the amount you need today, and try to find more for tomorrow. Reduce your activity level to minimize your body's water requirements.

Consider some of these hidden sources of water in your home: melted ice cubes, water drained from the water heater faucet, and liquids from canned fruits and vegetables. As a last resort, you can use the water in your toilet's reservoir tank (not the bowl).

If your neighborhood has been affected by a broken water or sewage line or a failure at the water treatment plant, shut off your home's water line to prevent contaminated water from entering.

Finding usable water outside your home   In an emergency, you may need to gather water from a source outside your home. If you can, collect rainwater. Also consider bodies of moving water such as streams, rivers, ponds, lakes, and natural springs.

Avoid water that is likely to be contaminated. This includes standing water, and water with any floating matter, odor, or dark color. Never drink floodwater. Use saltwater only if you distill it first.

Purifying water outside of your home   If you must use an outside source of water, always purify it before using it for drinking, food preparation, or hygiene. The two easiest purification methods are boiling and disinfecting. While these methods will kill most microbes, they won't remove other contaminants like metals, salts, and most chemicals.

Before purifying water, let any suspended particles settle to the bottom, or strain the water through layers of paper towel, a coffee filter, or a clean cloth. Then bring the water to a rolling boil for 3-5 minutes, or disinfect it with liquid bleach using the technique previously described for water storage.

You may want to consider purchasing or building a DIY (do it yourself) gravity water purification system. Follow these instructions to build a portable water purification system easily and inexpensively:

Purchase ceramic filter candles online and two 5-gallon buckets with lids from your local home improvement store. Loosely place a lid on top of one bucket. (Do not press down to seal the lid.) Place the un-lidded second bucket on top of the loosely-lidded first bucket. Using a 1/2-inch drill bit, drill a hole through the bottom of the top bucket and the lid of the bottom bucket. Remove the nut from the filter candle, and insert the threaded end of the filter into the drilled hole in bottom of the bucket and lid. Replace the nut, and hand tighten. Do not insert the candle filter until ready to use. To store, stack the buckets with extra filters inside, stack the lids on top, and label as "Water Purifier." Follow diagrams on next page.

DIY Gravity Water Purification System Diagrams

Below are very simple diagrams to assemble your own gravity purification system. It works just like the gravity systems that are very expensive.

Ceramic water filter candle.

Two 5 gal. buckets with lids.

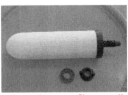

Drill 1/2 in. hole in
the center of lid.

Drill 1/2 in. hole in the center
of the bottom of one bucket.

Insert water filter into bottom of bucket through the hole.

(continued next page)

There are several different types of water candle filters online by different companies. They will filter up to 100 to 3000 gallons through one filter. I would pay the extra to get the ones that filter more gallons per filter.

Attach lid with hole to bottom.

Gently tighten nut.

Place bucket and attached lid on top of second bucket.

Ready to use.

To use your water filter, simply pour the water to be filtered into top bucket. The water will drip through the filter to the bottom bucket. Because it is a gravity flow it is a slow process.

11
Sprouting And Storing Seeds

Our body's first defense against free radicals is antioxidants, and there's no better source of antioxidants than sprouted seeds! The nutritional value of seeds dramatically increases once they've sprouted. Sprouts are delicious, healthy, and inexpensive, and sprouting is an easy process.

Reasons for sprouting   Sprouts are a fabulous addition to your diet because they are:

- **Inexpensive.** One tablespoon of seeds will produce about a quart of sprouts.

- **Quick and simple to grow** . You can grow and prepare sprouts in less than a minute per day! They grow in all seasons and nearly anywhere indoors. They require very little space.

- **Fresh and ready, fast.** When you sprout, you're truly creating a garden in your kitchen with minimal effort. No digging, planting, weeding, pests, or chemicals are required! You'll have a bountiful, nutrition-packed harvest in just a few days, and your sprouts will stay fresh in your refrigerator for days or even weeks if rinsed properly.

- **A complete, highly nutritious food source** . Sprouts are real, living health food. Several varieties contain more protein than cooked meat at a tiny fraction of the cost, and the balance of amino acids makes this protein much more digestible. All sprouts are rich in vitamins, minerals, trace elements, enzymes, and fiber. When exposed to light, your sprouts will become greener and rich in chlorophyll.

• **Extremely delicious** . You may be surprised how tasty sprouts are! Enjoy them in salads, on sandwiches, stir-fried, steamed, in soups, or even baked in wholesome, homemade breads.

• **Low in fat and calories.** One fully-packed cup of alfalfa spouts contains only 16 calories! Sprouts are simple sugars for quick energy. They contain no cholesterol, and they provide several essential fatty acids.

• **A detox and digestion aid.** The chlorophyll in sprouts helps cleanse and oxygenate the blood, and the enzymes aid in the digestion and assimilation of nutrients. The fiber supports healthy elimination, and lecithin rids the body of cholesterol. Eating raw foods is one of the best ways to detox your body.

• **Immune system builders.** Sprouts are loaded with antioxidants which help the body to cleanse, detox, rebuild, and heal itself. Antioxidant enzymes are essential for the proper function of the immune system.

• **Note:** For the healthiest sprouts, use only organic, non-GMO seeds.

• *Types of seeds used in sprouting* Use any of the following seeds for sprouts: Alfalfa, mung bean, garbanzo, green pea, adzuki bean, radish seeds, green lentils, red lentils, blue lentils, broccoli, hard red wheat.

• *Combination seed mixes for storage and variety* The following seed combinations store well, taste great, and will add some welcomed variety to your diet:

- **Protein Power Mix:** Garbanzo, green pea, adzuki bean, and mung bean.

- **Super Salad Mix:** Broccoli, mung bean, radish, and alfalfa.

Note: Some seed are poisonous when sprouted. Stick to the list of healthy seeds above.

Storing seeds for sprouting   If you plan to sprout your seeds, store them in jars or in Mylar bags WITHOUT oxygen absorbers. Seeds used for sprouting or planting require oxygen to remain viable.

Recipes

12
Recipe Prep Guidelines

Recipe customization   The recipes in this book are not hard-and-fast rules! Feel free to customize them according to your family's dietary needs and preferences. Here are a few customization tips and ideas:

Omit meats and substitute vegetarian bouillon granules for beef/chicken bouillon to create vegetarian meals.

Increase or decrease ingredients according to your personal tastes.

When using vanilla you can add the amount called for and mix it with the amount of sugar in the recipe and let it air dry to add it into the other dry ingredients. Then you do not have to add liquid vanilla when preparing the recipe. I have already done this in some recipes.

Package the recipe with freeze-dried ingredients instead of using a fresh or canned add-in. Simply add a little extra liquid in the preparation. (Note: You must repackage freeze-dried meats in a completely dry environment within 48 hours of opening the can. Use oxygen absorbers to ensure an oxygen-free environment.)

Other tips for packaging recipes   When a recipe calls for some ingredients to be put in baggies, vacuum-seal each small baggy if possible. If you don't have a vacuum sealer, then use zip-seal baggies, but leave a small opening in the seal. This way, the oxygen absorber can also absorb the oxygen from the small baggy. Just be sure to position the baggy so that the ingredients won't spill out.

Use a canning funnel to fill jars and bags easily. When filling Mylar bags, prop the bag in a shallow box to prevent it from tipping.

Label your jars and bags with the recipe name

55

and preparation instructions. You can conveniently write the information on an adhesive address label and place the label on the bag or jar before filling.

Store your filled Mylar bags in a study bucket, and seal the bucket tightly with a lid. I like the orange Home Depot buckets. They're food-grade and heavy duty, and they're half the cost of most food-grade buckets.

Recipes labeled "JAW" are recipes you "Just Add Water" to when preparing.

Recipes labeled "NRLT" (Not Recommended for Long - Term Storage) contain ingredients with too much oil or moisture for safe long-term storage, for example grated parmesan cheese (not including dried or freeze-dried non-fat cheese) and raisins. Write an expiration date on the label for recipes with any type of oil/fat or moisture content. If you want to keep these recipes for long-term storage, you can omit the ingredients with oil/fat or moisture and add them to the "Add In" ingredients at the time of preparation, or substitute a non-fat powdered or freeze-dried version of the ingredient.

Always remember to discard the oxygen absorber before preparing the meal. If you are giving as gift jar be sure to include the removing of the oxygen absorber in the labeling.

Beverages

Breads

And

Breakfasts

Cafe Vienna Coffee (JAW)

Combine all ingredients, then blend 1 cup at a time in blender until the mixture is the consistency of a powder. Mix all together well. Store in jar or Mylar bag, and seal accordingly.

1/2 c instant coffee	1 t cinnamon
2/3 c sugar	1/4 c vanilla instant
1/2 c dry milk powder	pudding mix
1/4 c nondairy powdered creamer	

Directions: In a coffee cup, combine 2 tablespoons of mix and 3/4 cup of steaming hot water. Stir and serve.

Cookies-n-Cream Coffee (JAW)

Combine all ingredients, then blend 1 cup at a time in blender until the mixture is the consistency of a powder. Mix all together well. Store in jar or Mylar bag and seal accordingly.

1/2 c instant coffee	1 t cinnamon
2/3 c sugar	1/2 c powdered coffee
1/2 c dry milk powder	creamer
1 large box Jello Cookies-n-Cream flavored instant pudding mix (4.2 oz.)	

Directions: In a coffee cup, combine 3 level tablespoons of mix and 1 cup of steaming hot water. Stir and serve.

Cappuccino Coffee (JAW)

Combine all ingredients, then blend 1 cup at a time in blender until the mixture is the consistency of a powder. Mix all together well. Store in jar or Mylar bag, and seal accordingly.

1 c white sugar
1 t ground cinnamon
1/2 t ground nutmeg
2 c nondairy powdered
creamer or powdered French vanilla creamer

2 c instant chocolate drink mix
1-1/2 c instant coffee

Directions: In a coffee cup, combine 3 tablespoons of mix and 1 cup of steaming hot water. Stir and serve.

Fireside Coffee (JAW)

Combine all ingredients, then blend 1 cup at a time in blender until the mixture is the consistency of a powder. Mix all together well. Store in jar or Mylar bag, and seal accordingly.

2 c sugar
1-1/2 c instant coffee
1 c nondairy powdered
creamer

1/2 c cocoa powder
1/2 t ground cinnamon

Directions: In a coffee cup, combine 3 tablespoons of mix and 1 cup of steaming hot water. Stir and serve.

Instant Chai Tea (JAW)

Combine all ingredients in blender. Blend into a fine powder and mix well. Store in pint jar or Mylar bag.

2-1/2 c white sugar	1 c nonfat dry milk powder
2 t ground cinnamon	1 c powdered coffee
1 t ground cloves	creamer
1 t allspice	*1 c vanilla-flavored
2 t ground ginger	powdered coffee creamer
1 t nutmeg	
1-1/2 c unsweetened instant tea	

Directions: In a mug, pour steaming hot water over 2-3 heaping teaspoons of mix. For iced chai, combine slightly more mix with hot water, and then add ice.

*To substitute vanilla extract for the vanilla-flavored creamer, simply combine 2 teaspoons vanilla extract with the sugar and let dry. Break up any sugar lumps. Then add one extra cup of powdered coffee creamer, and blend as directed.

Cafe Swiss Mocha Coffee (JAW)

Combine all ingredients in blender. Blend into a fine powder and mix well. Store in pint jar or Mylar bag.

1-1/3 c sugar	1 c instant coffee
1 c non-dairy coffee	1/2 c cocoa powder
creamer	

Directions: In a coffee cup, combine 2 to 2-1/2 teaspoons of coffee mix with 1 cup boiling water. Stir and serve.

Homemade Hot Cocoa (JAW)

Combine all ingredients except marshmallows in blender. Blend into a fine powder and mix well. Stir in marshmallows. Store in pint jar or Mylar bag.

4 c powdered milk	1-1/2 c sugar
1 c cocoa powder	1/2 t salt
1 c nondairy powdered creamer	Dried marshmallows to taste (optional)

Directions: In a mug, combine 3-4 tablespoons of cocoa mix and 1 cup boiling water in mug. Stir and serve.

Friendship Tea (JAW)

Combine all ingredients, then blend 1 cup at a time in blender until the mixture is the consistency of a powder. Mix all together well. Store in jar or Mylar bag, and seal accordingly.

1 t ground cinnamon	2 c powdered orange drink
1 t ground cloves	1/2 c red cinnamon candy
1/3 c instant tea	(such as Red Hots)

Directions: In a mug, combine 1-1/2 tablespoons of mix and 1 cup hot water. Stir until the candies dissolve and serve.

Irish American Soda Bread Mix (NRLT) (JAW)

Layer ingredients in quart jar or Mylar bag and seal accordingly. Pack each layer into the container before adding the next ingredient.

3 c all-purpose flour	1 c raisins*
1/2 t salt	1/3 c of sugar
1 t baking soda	6 T butter powder
2 t baking powder	6 T buttermilk powder
1 t cinnamon	1 T dried egg white powder

Directions: Preheat oven to 350°. Empty contents into a bowl and mix well. Add 1-1/2 cup water to the dry ingredients, stirring until moistened. The batter should be stiff and sticky. Pour batter into a greased 5 x 9 inch loaf pan. Bake for 45 to 50 minutes.

*For long term storage omit raisins and add in when preparing the recipe.

Indian Flat Bread

Mix all dry ingredients well. Put in pint jar or Mylar bag, seal accordingly.

1 2/3 c all-purpose flour	1/3 c powdered milk
2/3 T baking powder	1 t herbs (optional)
1/2 t salt	1/4 t garlic powder (optional)

(continued next page)

Add-In: 1/2 T olive oil
extra oil for cooking

Directions: Pour flour mixture into bowl, add olive oil, and slowly add 2/3 cup of water while kneading the dough. You should end up with stiff workable dough that is not sticky. If it is wet and sticky you need to add more flour. If the dough will not hold together then you need more water. Put dough in plastic wrap and let it rest a few hours. Then divide dough into small balls and flatten into 1/8 inch patties. Fry over medium heat with small amount of oil until light golden brown like you would pancakes. Makes 4-6.

Texas Corn Bread

Mix all ingredients well and store in Mylar Bag or jar and seal accordingly.

1 c cornmeal	1/2 t salt
1 c all-purpose flour	1/3 c white sugar
2 t baking powder	5 T dried powdered milk
2 t dried egg whites	

Add-In: 1/4 c canola oil

Directions: Preheat oven to 400°. Grease muffin pan or line with paper muffin liners. Pour mix into bowl. Add oil and 1 cup water; stir well. Spoon batter into prepared muffin cups. Bake for 15 to 20 minutes, or until a toothpick inserted into a muffin comes out clean.

Country Biscuit

Mix all ingredients well and store in Mylar Bag or jar and seal accordingly.

2 c all-purpose flour   1/4 t salt
1/2 t cream of tartar   2 t white sugar
1 T baking powder   5 T dried powdered milk

Add-In: 1/2 c melted butter or canola oil

Directions: Preheat oven to 450°. Put mix into bowl, stir in butter/oil and 1 cup water just until moistened. Drop batter on a lightly greased cookie sheet by the tablespoon. Bake in preheated oven until golden, about 8 to 12 minutes. Makes about

Raisin Oat Bran Muffin Mix

Mix all ingredients and put in Mylar bag, or layer in a wide mouth quart jar and seal accordingly. Firmly pack each layer before adding next ingredient.

2 c oat bran   1 T baking powder
1 c raisins*   1 t cinnamon
1/4 c buttermilk powder   1/2 t salt
 4 t dried egg white   1 c flour
1/2 c white sugar

Add-In: 1/3 c oil

Empty jar into a large mixing bowl. Blend dry ingredients thoroughly. Add 1/3 cup oil and 1 cup water. Mix until just blended. Don't over mix. Grease a muffin pan or line with paper muffin liners. Fill muffin cups 3/4 full. Bake at 425° for 15 minutes. Makes about 15 muffins.

(continued next page)

*For long term storage omit the raisins and add in when preparing the recipe.

Chocolate Chip Muffin Mix

Mix all ingredients and put in Mylar bag. If using a quart jar, mix first three ingredients and put in bottom of jar, and layer the remaining ingredients.

2-1/4 c all-purpose flour   1/4 c brown sugar*
3 t baking powder   1/2 c white sugar
1/2 t salt   5 T dried powder milk
1 c semi-sweet chocolate   4 t dried egg white
    chips*

Add-In: 1/3 c vegetable oil, 1 t vanilla

Directions: Preheat oven to 375°. Prepare 12 muffin cups with cooking spray or paper muffin liners. Empty the mix into a large bowl and stir to combine. In a separate bowl, whisk together 1 cup water, oil, and vanilla. Add the wet ingredients to the mix and stir until just moistened. Distribute the batter evenly into muffin cups. Bake for 20 to 25 minutes until a toothpick inserted into a muffin comes out clean. Makes 12 muffins.

*For long term storage omit the chocolate chips and the brown sugar, add in when preparing the recipe.

Ginger Spice Muffins

Place ingredients in jar or Mylar bag. Label and seal accordingly.

(continued next page)

1 3/4 c flour
3 t baking powder
1/2 t baking soda
1/2 t salt
1/3 c powdered milk

1/2 t ground nutmeg
1/4 t ground ginger
1/4 t ground cloves
1 T powder egg white
2 T vanilla sugar*

*To make vanilla sugar, add 1 teaspoon of vanilla to 2 tablespoons of sugar mix well and let air dry thoroughly and break up into granules before using in recipe. Or you can omit the vanilla in the recipe and add it to the "Add-In" in liquid form when you prepare the recipe. Be sure to add it to your label.

Combine all the ingredients in a medium bowl. Store the mixture in an airtight container. Attach these written instructions to the jar.

Add-In: 1/4 cup butter, melted
1 t vanilla (if it is omitted from the recipe)

Directions: Preheat the oven to 400 degrees F, and grease 12 muffin tins. In a large bowl, combine the muffin mix with the butter and 1 cup water. Stir until the ingredients are blended. The batter will be lumpy. Fill muffin tins 2/3 full, and bake for 15 minutes. Makes 12 muffins.

Buttermilk Pancake Mix

Combine all ingredients and put in jar or Mylar bag and seal accordingly.

1-1/2 t baking soda	1/4 c dried buttermilk powder
3 t baking powder	3/4 t nutmeg
3 c flour	2 t dried egg white
3/4 t salt	1 T sugar (optional)

Add-In: 1 T oil

Directions: Combine 1 cup pancake mix, 1 cup water, and 1 tablespoon oil. With a 1/4 cup measure, ladle onto hot, oiled griddle and cook each side until golden brown. Top with your favorite toppings. Serves 2.

Sausage & Egg Skillet Breakfast (JAW)

Combine egg mixture ingredients in a small baggy. Place the baggy in jar or Mylar bag. Combine sausage and potato mixture ingredients, and add to the jar or bag. Seal accordingly.

Sausage and potato mixture:

1 c freeze dried sausage	1 t seasoning salt
2 c dehydrated diced potatoes	

Egg mixture:

1/3 c OvaEasy egg crystals	1/2 t dried onion flakes
1/3 c dried bell peppers	1/4 t dried garlic granules
2 T freeze dried mushrooms	1/4 t seasoning salt
1/3 c freeze dried shredded cheese	1 t Italian herbs

(continued next page)

Directions: In large non-stick skillet, combine the sausage and potato mixture with 4 cup boiling water. Cover for 15 minutes or until potatoes are tender. Drain. Cook 10-15 minutes over medium heat, stirring once or twice, allowing the potatoes to brown. Do not over stir. In separate bowl, combine the egg mixture with 2/3 cup cool water, whisking well. Allow to sit for 5 minutes. Add egg mixture to the potatoes and sausage, and continue cooking until eggs are done. Makes about five 3/4 c servings.

Spiced Cream Of Wheat (JAW)

Combine ingredients in a pint jar or in small Mylar bag and seal accordingly.

1/4 c powder milk	1/8 t cinnamon
1/3 c sugar	1/8 t nutmeg
1 T butterscotch or vanilla	1/2 c cream-of-wheat
instant pudding	

Conventional directions: Boil 2 cup water in a small saucepan. Add contents of package and cook 3-4 minutes.

Microwave directions: Combine package contents with 1-1/4 cup water, and microwave on high for 2 minutes. Stir, and cook 1 additional minute. Makes four 1/2 cup servings.

Instant Breakfast Drink (JAW)

Combine all ingredients in jars or Mylar bags, and seal accordingly.

2 - 3 oz. boxes instant vanilla or chocolate pudding
12 c instant dry milk powder

2/3 c sugar
4 t vanilla powder*
24 scoops powdered protein

*Vanilla flavored protein powder can be substituted for the vanilla powder.

Directions: Mix 1 cup of ice water and 2/3 cup of instant breakfast mix until lumps dissolve.

Single Instant Oatmeal Packets (JAW)

For each oatmeal packet, place all ingredients in a snack-size zipper bag. For long-term storage, seal in a small Mylar bag.

1/4 c quick cooking oats
1 t powdered milk
1/4 t cinnamon (optional)
Freeze-dried blueberries (optional)

1/8 t salt
1 T sugar (optional)

Conventional directions: Empty packet into bowl. Add 1/2 cup boiling water. Stir and let stand for 2 minutes.

Microwave directions: Empty packet into microwave-safe bowl. Add 1/2 cup water and microwave approximately 1 minute or until done. Adjust water amount for thicker or thinner oatmeal.

Instant Oatmeal – Bulk (JAW)

Mix all ingredients and store in quart jar or Mylar bag, and seal accordingly.

3 c quick cooking oats	1/3 c sugar (optional)
1/2 c powdered milk	3/4 t salt
1 t ground cinnamon	

Directions: Mix 2/3 cup of dry mixture with 1 cup boiling water in a bowl. Stir to remove lumps. Let stand 1-2 minutes and serve.

Note: Mix well before each serving. Ingredients will separate.

Hot Rice Cereal Mix (JAW)

Layer in pint jar, or combine and seal in a Mylar bag. For long term storage leave the raisins out.

1 c long grain white rice	1/2 c sugar
1/4 c dried powdered milk	1/16 t nutmeg
1 t ground cinnamon	1/4 c raisins

Directions: Add contents of jar to 2-3/4 cup of water in medium sauce pan and bring to boil. Lower heat and cover. Simmer 15-25 minutes, stirring occasionally or until all water is absorbed and rice is tender. Serve with milk or cream.

Storing Bulk Oatmeal, Rice, and Other Grains

Using quart jars or Mylar bags, label with cooking directions from original packaging, and seal accordingly.

Instant Cream of Wheat Single Packets

Place ingredients in a single size jar or Mylar bag and seal accordingly

1/4 c instant cream of wheat	3 T powdered milk
1 T sugar (more if needed)	1/8 t cinnamon

Directions: Pure packet of cereal into a cereal bowl, boil 1 cup of water add to cereal, cover for 10 minutes and serve. Single serving.

Salad Dressings
And
Dips Mixes

Italian Salad Dressing Mix

Combine all ingredients. Place in a small jar or Mylar bag, and seal accordingly. (Recipe may be doubled.)

2 T garlic salt   2 t dried basil
2 T onion powder   2 T dried parsley
1/4 c dried oregano   1/2 t celery salt
2 t ground black pepper   1/4 c salt
1/2 t dried thyme

Add-In: 1/4 c vinegar of choice
2/3 c oil of choice

Directions: Whisk together vinegar, oil, 2 tablespoons water, and 2 tablespoons of dressing mix. Also makes a great marinade.

French Italian Salad Dressing Mix

Combine all ingredients. Place in a small jar or Mylar bag, and seal accordingly.

3/4 c granulated sugar   2 t paprika
3 t salt   2 t dried oregano
1/2 t black pepper   1/2 t dry garlic granules
2 t dry mustard   6 t dry onion flakes

Add-In: 1/2 c oil of choice
1/4 c vinegar of choice
1/2 c ketchup

Directions: Whisk together oil, vinegar, ketchup, and 1/4 cup of dressing mix. Let stand at room temperature 5 hrs. Chill 30 minutes before serving. Also makes a great marinade.

Caesar Salad Dressing Mix

Combine all ingredients. Place in a small jar or Mylar bag, and seal accordingly. (Single recipe packet.)

1-1/2 t grated lemon peel   1/2 t pepper
1/8 t garlic powder   1 t oregano
2 T dried grated
Parmesan cheese

Add-In: 1/2 c oil of choice
1/4 c lemon juice

Directions: Combine oil, lemon juice, 1 tablespoon water, and dressing mix in a glass jar. Cover and shake until well blended. Refrigerate before serving.

Tangy Salad Dressing

Combine all ingredients. Place in a small jar or Mylar bag, and seal accordingly. (Recipe may be doubled.)

1 c powered milk   1 t garlic powder
1/4 c sugar   1 t salt
4 t dried basil flakes   2 t dried mustard
4 t dried onion flakes

Add-In: 1 t lemon Juice
3/4 c mayonnaise

Direction: Whisk together lemon juice, 1/2 cup water, and 1/4 cup of dressing mix. Whisk in mayonnaise. Mix well before serving. Makes about 1 cup.

Buttermilk Ranch Dressing & Dip Mix

Combine all ingredients. Place in small jar or Mylar bag, and seal accordingly.

4 T buttermilk powder	1/2 t oregano
2 T dried parsley	1/4 t paprika
1 T dried chives	1/4 t salt
1 t garlic powder	1/4 t seasoning salt
2 T dried minced onion	1/4 t black pepper
1 t dried celery flakes	1/4 t dried dill weed
	(optional)

Dressing Add-In: 1/2 c mayonnaise

Dip Add-In: 1 c mayonnaise
1 c sour cream

Dressing Directions: Whisk together mayonnaise, 1/2 cup water, and 1 tablespoon dressing mix. Chill 1 hour before serving.

Dip Directions: Mix well mayonnaise, sour cream, and 2 tablespoons dressing mix. Chill 4 hours before serving.

Herb Dressing Mix

Combine all ingredients. Place in small jar or Mylar bag and seal accordingly.

1/4 c dry parsley	1/4 t garlic powder
2 T dry oregano, crumbled	1 T fennel seeds, crushed
2 T basil, crumbled	1 T dry mustard
2 T marjoram, crumbled	1-1/2 t black pepper
2 T sugar	

(continued next page)

Add In: 1/4 c vinegar
2/3 c oil

Directions: Whisk together vinegar, oil, 2 tablespoons water, and 1 tablespoon dressing mix. For more robust flavor, add another 1/4-1/2 teaspoon dressing mix. Let stand at room temperature for 30 minutes.

Dip Mixes

The dip mixes on the following pages are delicious! Serve them with your favorite crackers, fresh vegetables, or a variety of chips. To create a flavorful cheese spread for bagels, crackers, or breads, prepare the recipes with softened cream cheese instead of mayo and sour cream. Be creative! The recipes are guidelines - not commandments! You can add a little more or less of any ingredient to create your own custom flavors.

For long-term storage, I recommend using a 100 cc oxygen absorber in each jar or Mylar bag, and then seal.

Most of the dip recipes are not good for bulk storage because the herbs, salts, and granules will settle unevenly. Just make single-serving portions as directed. The recipes that are labeled "Bulk" are good for bulk storage. Prepare them for storage in the larger quantities as directed. When you're ready to make the dip, just be sure to follow the directions below the ingredients list for single-serving preparation.

Parmesan Dip Mix

Combine all ingredients. Place in small jar or Mylar bag, and seal accordingly.

1 T dried parsley
1 t dried basil
1 t garlic powder
1/2 t dried onion flakes

1/2 t dried oregano
1/4 t dried thyme
1/4 t seasoning salt
Dash black pepper

Add-In: 1 c sour cream
1 c mayonnaise
3 T dried Parmesan
 cheese

Directions: In a medium bowl, combine contents of jar or bag with sour cream and mayonnaise. Mix well. Cover and chill approximately 8 hours before serving.

Onion Dip Mix

Combine all ingredients. Place in small jar or Mylar bag, and seal accordingly.

2 T dried onion flakes
1/4 t garlic powder
1 T beef or vegetable
bouillon granules

3/4 t dried parsley
3/4 t onion powder
1 t dried chives

Add-In: 2 c sour cream

Directions: In a medium bowl, combine contents of jar or bag with sour cream. Mix well. Cover and chill approximately 1 hour before serving.

Italian Dip Mix

Combine all ingredients. Place in small jar or Mylar bag, and seal accordingly.

4 T Parmesan cheese   1 t seasoning salt
3 t garlic powder   1 t dried basil
2 t onion powder   1 t dried oregano

Add-In: 2 c sour cream

Directions: In a medium bowl, combine contents of jar or bag with sour cream. Mix well. Cover and chill approximately 2 hours before serving.

Fiesta Mexican Dip Mix

Combine all ingredients. Place in small jar or Mylar bag, and seal accordingly.

1 T chili powder   3/4 t dried cilantro
1 t garlic powder   1/8 t cayenne pepper
1 t onion powder   1/4 t seasoning salt
1 T dried green/red   3 t dried parsley
bell peppers

Add-In: 1 c sour cream
1 c mayonnaise

Directions: In a medium bowl, combine contents of jar or bag with sour cream and mayonnaise. Mix well. Cover and chill approximately 8 hours before serving.

Dill Dip Mix (Bulk Recipe)

Combine all ingredients. Place in small jar or Mylar bag, and seal accordingly.

1/4 c dried dill weed   1/4 c dried onion flakes
1/4 c Accent   1/2 c dried parsley flakes
1/4 c seasoning salt

Add-In: 1 c sour cream
1 c mayonnaise

Directions: In a medium bowl, combine 3 tablespoons of dip mix with sour cream and mayonnaise. Chill 2 hours to allow the flavors to blend. Serve with fresh vegetables or chips.

Herb & Garlic Dip Mix

Combine all ingredients. Place in small jar or Mylar bag, and seal accordingly.

2 t garlic powder   2 t dried onion flakes
1 t seasoning salt   1 T dried parsley
2 t dried tarragon   1 T dried thyme

Add-In: 2 c sour cream

Directions: In a medium bowl, combine contents of jar or bag with sour cream. Mix well. Chill 3-4 hours before serving.

Bacon Flavored Dip Mix (Bulk Recipe)

Combine all ingredients. Place in small jar or Mylar bag, and seal accordingly.

8 T imitation bacon bits
4 T instant minced onion

4 t instant beef bouillon
1/2 t dried minced garlic

Add-In: 1 cup sour cream

Directions: In a medium bowl, combine 3 tablespoons of dip mix with sour cream. Chill 1 hour before serving.

Variations: Substitute 1 cup yogurt, 1 cup cottage cheese, or 1 package softened cream cheese (8 oz.) for sour cream.

Garlic Chive Dip Mix

Combine all ingredients. Place in small jar or Mylar bag, and seal accordingly.

2 t garlic powder
1 t seasoning salt
1 t dried celery flakes

4 t dried chives
2 t dried onion flakes
2 t dried parsley flakes

Add-In: 2 c sour cream

Directions: In a medium bowl, combine contents of jar or bag with sour cream. Mix well. Chill 2-3 hours before serving.

Buttermilk Ranch Dip & Dressing Mix

Combine all ingredients. Place in small jar or Mylar bag, and seal accordingly.

4 T buttermilk powder	1/2 t oregano
2 T dried parsley	1/4 t paprika
1 T dried chives	1/4 t salt
1 t garlic powder	1/4 t seasoning salt
2 T dried minced onion	1/4 t black pepper
1 t dried celery flakes	1/4 t dried dill weed
	(optional)

Dip Add-In: 1 c mayonnaise
1 c sour cream

Dressing Add-In: 1/2 c mayonnaise

Dressing Directions: Whisk together mayonnaise, 1/2 cup water, and 1 tablespoon dressing mix. Chill 1 hour before serving.

Dip Directions: Mix well mayonnaise, sour cream, and 2 tablespoons dressing mix. Chill 4 hours before serving.

Seasoning Blends
And
Gravy Mixes

Taco Seasoning Blend

Combine all ingredients well. Place in jar or Mylar bag, and seal accordingly.

4 t chili powder
1/2 t dried oregano
1 t cornstarch
2 t garlic powder

2 t crushed red pepper
2 t ground cumin
4 t salt

Chili Seasoning Blend

Combine all ingredients well. Place in jar or Mylar bag, and seal accordingly.

4 t chili powder
1 T crushed red pepper
1 T dried minced onion
1 T dried, minced garlic
2 t white sugar
1/4 c all-purpose flour
(optional for thickness)

2 t ground cumin
2 t dried parsley
2 t salt
1 t dried basil
1/4 t black pepper

Pasta Salad Seasoning

Combine all ingredients well. Place in jar or Mylar bag, and seal accordingly.

2 t salt
1/2 t garlic salt
1 T instant minced onion
2 T parsley flakes
1/2 c sesame seed

1/2 t dried dill seed
2 T poppy seeds
3 T celery seeds
2 t paprika
1/2 t ground pepper

Garlic Bread Seasoning Blend

Combine all ingredients well. Place in jar or Mylar bag, and seal accordingly.

6 T garlic powder

2 T parsley

2 T oregano

2 T basil

2 T marjoram

2 T salt

Note: This blend is excellent on shrimp scampi too.   You can also add Parmesan cheese when preparing.

Italian Seasoning Blend

Combine all ingredients well. Place in jar or Mylar bag, and seal accordingly.

2 T dried oregano

2 T dried basil

1 T dried thyme

1 T dried parsley

1 T dried marjoram

1-1/2 t dried rosemary

1-1/2 t garlic powder

Creole Seasoning Blend

Combine all ingredients well. Place in jar or Mylar bag, and seal accordingly.

1 T onion powder

1 T dried oregano

1 T dried thyme

1 T cayenne pepper

1 T salt

1 T pepper

2-1/2 T paprika

2 T garlic powder

Blackened Seasoning Blend

Combine all ingredients well. Place in jar or Mylar bag, and seal accordingly.

1 T paprika	1 t onion powder
3/4 t cayenne pepper	1 t garlic powder
1 t salt	1/2 t dried thyme
1 t black pepper	dash cumin
1/2 t dried oregano	

Gravy Mixes
Granny's White Gravy (JAW)

Combine all ingredients. Place in pint jar or Mylar bag, and seal accordingly.

3/4 c butter powder	1 t salt
1 c dry milk powder	1/2 t pepper
3/4 c all-purpose white flour	

Directions: In medium saucepan, whisk together 1 cup water and 1/2 cup gravy mix until smooth. Cook on low heat until thickened, stirring constantly to prevent burning. If sauce becomes too thick, whisk in small amounts of water until gravy is the desired consistency.

Veggie Flavored Gravy Mix (JAW)

Combine all ingredients. Place in pint jar or Mylar bag, and seal accordingly.

1 T dried thyme flakes	1 t black pepper
1 T dried parsley flakes	3 c of all-purpose flour
3/4 c dried minced onions	
3/4 c vegetable bouillon	
granules	(continued next page)

Directions: In medium saucepan, whisk together 1-1/2 cups water and 6 tablespoons gravy mix. Cook on medium heat until thickened, stirring frequently to prevent burning.

Beef Gravy Mix (JAW)

Combine all ingredients. Place in pint jar or Mylar bag, and seal accordingly.

1-2/3 c cornstarch	1/2 t black pepper
2 t onion powder	4 t instant coffee crystals
6 T beef bouillon granules	1 t garlic powder

Directions: Measure 3 tablespoons gravy mix into a medium saucepan. Add 1-1/2 cups water and bring to boil. Reduce heat and simmer 1 minute.

Creamy Chicken Gravy Mix (JAW)

Combine all ingredients. Place in pint jar or Mylar bag, and seal accordingly.

1/2 t pepper	1-1/2 t turmeric (optional)
1 c butter powder	3 t onion powder (optional)
2-2/3 c dry milk powder	1-1/2 t garlic powder
1/2 c chicken bouillon granules	(optional)
1-1/2 c all-purpose white flour	

Directions: In medium saucepan, whisk together 1 cup water and 1/2 cup gravy mix until smooth. Cook on low heat until thickened, stirring constantly to prevent burning. If sauce becomes too thick, whisk in small amounts of water until gravy is the desired consistency.

Chicken Flavored Gravy Mix (JAW)

Combine all ingredients. Place in pint jar or Mylar bag, and seal accordingly.

3 c all-purpose flour
3/4 c chicken bouillon granules
3/4 c dried minced onions

1 T dried thyme flakes
1 T dried parsley flakes
1 t black pepper

Directions: In medium saucepan, whisk together 1-1/2 cups water and 6 tablespoons gravy mix. Cook on low heat until thickened, stirring constantly to prevent burning. If sauce becomes too thick, whisk in small amounts of water until gravy is the desired consistency.

Soups

Chicken Tortilla Soup

Combine all ingredients. Place in quart jar or Mylar bag. Shake down ingredients to create more space if necessary. Seal accordingly.

1/2 c long-grain rice   1 t granulated garlic
2 T chicken bouillon granules   1 t ground cumin
1/8 t black pepper   1/4 c dried minced
1 t dried cilantro leaves   onion

Add-In: 1 can diced tomatoes (10 oz.)
1 small can green chilies
1 can corn (15 oz.)
1 can chicken (5 oz.)
Tortilla chips

Directions: In a large stock pot, combine contents of jar or bag with 8 cups water. Add diced tomatoes, chilies, and corn. Bring to boil. Reduce heat to low. Cover and simmer 20 minutes. Stir in chicken and a few handfuls of tortilla chips. Cover and simmer 5 more minutes. Serve with tortilla chips or crackers. Makes 8 servings.

Fall Bean Soup

Layer beans in quart jar or Mylar bag. Combine spice ingredients in a small baggy, and place the baggy in the jar or Mylar bag. Seal accordingly.

1/2 c kidney beans   1/2 c red lentils
1/2 c split yellow peas   1/2 c small red bean
1/2 c black beans   1/2 c split green peas

(continued next page)

Spice Baggy:

1 t celery seed	3 t dried minced onion
1 t dried parsley flakes	1 t dried thyme
1 t seasoning salt	1 t garlic powder
1/4 t black pepper	2 bay leaves
3 t chicken bouillon granules	

Add-In: 1 can of chicken (5 oz.) (optional)
2 cans diced tomato (14-1/2 oz. each) un-drained

Directions: Rinse beans. In a large stock pot, cover beans with 4-6 cups of water and soak overnight. Drain and rinse. In the same stock pot, cover beans with 8 cups water, and bring to boil. Reduce heat to low. Cover and simmer approximately 1-1/2 hours or until beans are almost tender. Add tomatoes, chicken (if using), and contents of spice baggy. Cover and simmer 30 minutes, stirring occasionally. Uncover beans and continue simmering 1 hour longer or until beans are tender and soup thickens. Remove bay leaves before serving. Makes 10 servings.

Northern Country Soup

Layer all ingredients in wide mouth jar or Mylar bag, and seal accordingly.

1/2 c barley	2 T dried parsley
1/2 c dried split peas	2 T dried celery flakes
1/2 c uncooked white rice	2 t salt
1/2 c dry lentils	1/2 t lemon pepper
2 T dried minced onion	1-1/2 c macaroni
2 T beef bouillon granules	

Add-In: 2 cans of diced tomatoes (15oz), un-drained
1 cup of shredded cabbage (optional)
Directions: In a large stock pot, combine contents of jar

or bag with tomatoes, cabbage (if using), and 3 quarts water. Cover and simmer over medium-low heat 1-2 hours or until beans are tender.

Creamy Potato Soup (JAW)

Combine all ingredients well. Place in quart jar or Mylar bag, and seal accordingly.

1-1/2 c dry milk	1/4 t dried thyme
2 t instant chicken bouillon	1/8 t turmeric
2 t dried minced onion	1/4 t black pepper
1 t dried parsley	1-1/2 t seasoning salt
1-3/4 c instant mashed potatoes	

Single-Serving Directions: In a soup bowl, combine 1/2 cup soup mix with 1 cup boiling water. Stir and let stand 2-3 minutes. If you prefer a thinner soup, stir in small amounts of water at a time until the consistency is to your liking. One quart jar makes eight or nine 1-cup servings.

Chicken Noodle Soup

Layer ingredients in quart jar or Mylar bag in the order listed. Shake the ingredients down and/or gently break the noodles to create more space if necessary. Seal accordingly.

4 c wide egg noodles	1 t dried chives
2 T dried minced onion	2 t dried celery flakes
3 T chicken bouillon	1/4 t black pepper

(continued next page)

Add In: 1 can chicken (5 oz.) (optional)
1 can mixed vegetables or carrots (optional)

Note: Can add dehydrated carrots and freeze dried chicken to package instead of the "Add In's" and have the whole meal in one packet and then just add water when preparing recipe.

Directions: In a large stock pot, boil 8-10 cups water. Add contents of jar or bag. Lower heat to medium, and simmer until noodles are soft. Add canned chicken and vegetables (if using) and cook until heated through. Serve with bread or crackers. Makes 8-10 servings.

Onion Soup Mix (JAW)

Combine all ingredients well. Place in quart jar or Mylar bag, and seal accordingly.

2 t cornstarch	1/3 c instant onion flakes
1 t beef bouillon granules	2 dashes black pepper
3 t vegetable bouillon granules	

Soup Directions: Empty contents of jar or bag into a medium pot, and gradually stir in 4 cups cold water. When fully combined, bring the mixture to boil. Reduce heat to low. Cover and simmer 20 minutes. Makes four 1-cup servings.

Onion Dip Directions: In a medium bowl, combine contents of jar or bag with 2 cups sour cream. Chill before serving.

Split Pea Soup (JAW)

Combine all ingredients well. Place in pint jar or Mylar bag, and seal accordingly.

1/2 c green split peas	1 T dried celery flakes
1/2 c lentils	1/4 t dried thyme
1/2 c pearl barley	1 T cup parsley flakes
1/2 c macaroni	1/8 t salt
2 T dried onion flakes	1/8 t black pepper

Directions: In a large stock pot, combine contents of jar or bag with 8 cups water. Bring to boil. Reduce heat to low Cover and simmer gently for 45-60 minutes, or until peas are tender.

Loaded Hamburg Stew

Place all ingredients in a quart jar or Mylar bag in the order listed, and seal accordingly.

2-1/2 c pasta spirals	2 T beef bouillon granules
1 T dried parsley	2 t powered garlic
2 T dried celery	1 t dried thyme flakes
2 T dried onion flakes	

Add-In: 1/2 lb. ground beef
1 can diced tomatoes (14 oz.), un-drained
1 can corn
1 can carrots
1 can diced potatoes

Directions: In a large stock pot, brown ground beef. Add 10 cups water and bring to boil. Add contents of jar or bag and boil about 6 to 10 minutes longer until pasta is tender. Reduce heat to low. Stir in canned tomatoes, corn, carrots, and potatoes. Simmer 20 minutes. Makes 8-10 servings.

Beef Barley Soup Mix

Place barley and lentils in pint jar or Mylar bag. Combine spices in a baggy, and place the baggy in the jar or Mylar bag with the barley and lentils. Seal accordingly.

3/4 c medium pearl barley   1/2 c dried lentils

Spice Baggy:

1/4 c dried minced onions   1/2 t dried basil
3 t instant beef bouillon   1/2 t dried oregano
2 t dried celery flakes   1/4 t dried minced garlic
2 t dried parsley flakes   1/4 t black pepper
1/2 t dried thyme   2 bay leaves

Add-In: 1 can diced tomatoes (14 oz.), un-drained
1 can of peas (15 oz.) (optional)
Cooked boneless beef, burger, or steak

Directions: In a large stock pot, combine contents of jar or bag with 12 cups water. Stir in contents of spice baggy, canned tomatoes, and meat. Bring to boil. Reduce heat to low. Cover and simmer 1-1/2 to 1-3/4 hours or until lentils are tender. Add canned peas (if using) and cook until heated through. Remove bay leaves. Makes 8-10 servings.

Three Bean Chili Mix

Layer beans in quart jar or Mylar bag. Combine spices in a baggy, and place the baggy in the jar or Mylar bag with the beans. Seal accordingly.

1 c dried pink beans   1 c kidney beans
1 c dried red beans

(continued next page

Spice Baggy:

3 T chili powder	1 t oregano
2 T dried minced onions	2 T celery flakes
1 T garlic powder	2 T beef bouillon granules
2 T dried green/red bell peppers	2 T corn starch to thicken

Add In: 2 cans diced tomatoes (14 oz.), un-drained
1 can tomato sauce (8 oz.)
1 lb. ground beef or ground turkey, cooked and drained

Directions: In a large stock pot, soak beans overnight in about 6 cups water. Rinse and return to stock pot. Add 12 cups water and contents of spice baggy. Bring to boil. Reduce heat to low. Cover and simmer approximately 1-1/2 hours, until beans are tender. Add canned tomatoes, tomato sauce, and beef or turkey. Simmer 20 minutes to blend flavors. Makes 8-10 servings.

Rice & Lentil Soup Mix

Layer all ingredients in pint jar or Mylar bag, and seal accordingly. (Recipe may be doubled and stored in quart jar.)

1/3 c long-grain white rice	1/2 t ground black pepper
1/3 c green lentils	1 t poultry seasoning
1/3 c red lentils	1 T dried parsley
1 T celery flakes	
2 T chicken bouillon granules	

Add-In: 2 t butter
1 can of chicken (5 oz.) or fresh cooked chicken (optional)

(continued next page)

Directions: In a large stock pot, boil 8 cups water. Add butter, contents of jar or bag, and chicken (if using). Bring to boil. Reduce heat to medium, and simmer 30 minutes or until lentils and rice are tender.

Black Eyed Pea Soup Mix

Place peas in jar or Mylar bag. Combine spice ingredients in a baggy, and place the baggy in the jar or Mylar bag with the peas. Seal accordingly.

3-1/2 c dried black eyed peas

Spice Baggy:

1 t chili powder

1 t onion powder

1/2 t pepper

6 T chicken bouillon granules

1/2 c dried minced onion

2 T dried parsley flakes

2 t dried minced garlic

1/2 t garlic powder

Add-In: 2 cans diced tomatoes (14 oz. each)

Directions: Remove seasoning packet from jar or bag and set aside. Rinse peas. In a large stock pot, cover peas with water and let soak overnight. Drain and rinse peas. In the same pot, combine soaked peas with contents of spice baggy, tomatoes, and 12 cups water. Bring to boil. Reduce heat to low. Cover and simmer 1-1/2 hours or until peas are tender, stirring occasionally.

Creamy Rice & Chicken Soup Mix

Combine all ingredients. Place in quart jar or Mylar bag, and seal accordingly.

2 T dried parsley
3 T dried celery
3 T chicken bouillon
3/4 c dried chopped
 mushrooms

2 c white long-grain rice
2 T dried minced onion
1/2 c dry coffee creamer

Add-In: 1 can chicken (5 oz.)
1 can potatoes, chopped
1 can carrots

Directions: In a large stock pot, combine contents of jar or bag with 12 cups cold water. Cover and bring to boil over medium-high heat. Reduce heat and let simmer 25-35 minutes or until rice is tender. Add potatoes and carrots, and simmer five minutes. Makes 10-12 servings.

Black Bean Chili Mix

Place beans in quart jar or Mylar bag. Combine spice ingredients in a baggy, and place the baggy in the jar or Mylar bag with the beans. Seal accordingly.

3-1/4 c black beans

Spice Baggy:
3 T dried minced onion
2 T granulated garlic
1 t dried oregano
3 T chicken bouillon
 granules

2 T dried celery
2 t cumin
2 t dried cilantro
1/2 t cayenne pepper

(continued next page)

Add In: 1 can chicken (5 oz.)
1 large can diced tomatoes (28 oz.), un-drained

Directions: Remove baggy from jar or Mylar bag and set aside. Rinse beans. In a large stock pot, cover beans with 12 cups water and soak overnight. Drain beans. In same pot, cover beans again with 12 cups water. Bring to boil. Reduce heat to low and simmer for 1-1/2 hours. Add contents of spice baggy, chicken (if using), and tomatoes. Simmer 30-40 minutes longer. Makes 12 servings.

Friendship Soup

Layer all ingredients in wide mouth jar or Mylar bag, ending with tri-color pasta. Seal accordingly.

1/3 c long-grain white rice	1/4 c dried onion flakes
1/4 c barley	2 T dried celery flakes
1/2 c dry lentils	1/4 t black pepper
1/2 c dried split peas	1 t dried parsley
1 c uncooked tri-color macaroni	1/2 c uncooked twist spiral pasta
1/3 c beef bouillon granules	

Add-In: 1 lb. ground beef or diced stew beef
1 T olive oil

Directions: In a large stock pot, cook beef in olive oil. Remove tri-color pasta from top of jar or bag and set aside. Add the remaining contents to the pot with 12 cups water. Bring to boil. Reduce heat to medium-low and simmer 45 minutes. Add tri-color pasta and simmer 15 minutes or longer until pasta is tender. Makes 12 servings.

Minestrone Soup Mix

Layer all ingredients except beans in quart jar or Mylar bag. Combine beans in a baggy, and place the baggy in the jar with the other ingredients. Seal accordingly.

3 T beef bouillon granules   2 t dried basil
2 T dried onion flakes   1 T minced garlic
2 T dried celery   1/2 t black pepper
1/3 t thyme   2-1/4 c small pasta
2 T parsley flakes

Bean Baggy:
1/2 c kidney beans
1/2 c navy beans

Add-In: 1 large can diced tomatoes (28 oz.), un-drained

Directions: Remove beans from baggy and rinse thoroughly. In large stock pot, boil beans and 5 cups of water for 5 minutes over medium heat. Remove from heat and let stand for 1 hour. Drain beans. In same pot, cover beans again with 8 cups water and bring to boil. Reduce heat to low and simmer 1 hour. Add tomatoes and remaining contents of jar or bag, and simmer 45 minutes. Makes 8 servings.

Italian Bean Soup Mix

Combine or layer beans in jar or Mylar bag. Put pasta in a baggy. Combine spices in another baggy. Place baggies in jar or Mylar bag with beans, and seal accordingly.

1/2 c dried pinto beans   1/2 c dried kidney beans
1/2 c dried pink beans

Pasta Baggy:
1 c small pasta shells

Spice Baggy:
1 T dried parsley   1 t dried celery flakes
1 t dried oregano   2 t dried minced onion
1 t dried basil   1/2 t dried garlic powder
1 T chicken bouillon   1 t salt
granules

Add-In: 1 large can diced tomatoes (28 oz.), un-drained

Directions: Remove pasta and seasoning baggies and set aside. Rinse beans. In a large stock pot, cover beans with water and soak overnight. Rinse beans again and return to pot with 8 cups water, tomatoes, and contents of spice baggy. Bring to boil. Reduce heat to low. Cover and simmer 2 hours or until beans are tender. Uncover and increase heat to medium-low. Boil gently 35 minutes, stirring occasionally, until soup begins to thicken. Stir in pasta. Increase heat to medium and cook ten minutes longer or until pasta is tender.

Hearty Lentil & Wild Rice Soup Mix

Layer all ingredients in quart jar or Mylar bag, and seal accordingly.

3 c any color lentils	2 T dried minced onion
1/2 c wild rice	1 t dried thyme
1/4 c dried celery	1 t dried minced garlic
4 T chicken bouillon granules	
(continued next page)	

Add-Ins: 1 can diced tomatoes, un-drained
1 can of chicken or diced ham
Salt and pepper to taste

Directions: In a large stock pot, boil 16 cups water and contents of jar or bag. Reduce heat to low, and simmer 50-60 minutes or until rice and lentils are tender. Add tomatoes, chicken or ham, and salt and pepper. Simmer five minutes longer. Makes 16 one-cup servings.

Pen Pal Soup

Layer all ingredients in pint jar or Mylar bag, ending with alphabet pasta. Seal accordingly.

1/8 t black pepper	2 t dried Italian seasoning
1/2 t garlic powder	1/4 c pearl barley
1/2 c dry split peas	1/2 c dry lentils
1/4 c dried onion flakes	1/2 c uncooked long-grain white rice
2 t dried Italian seasoning	
1/3 c chicken bouillon granules	1/2 c uncooked alphabet pasta

(continued next page)

Add-In: 1 can diced tomatoes (un-drained)
1 can tomato paste (6 oz.)
1 can of chicken or 1 lb. cooked ground beef

Directions: Remove pasta from top of jar or bag and set aside. In large stock pot, combine and boil 12 cups water, tomatoes, tomato paste, chicken or beef, and remaining contents of jar or bag. Reduce heat to low. Cover and simmer 45 minutes. Stir in pasta. Cover and simmer 15-20 minutes longer or until pasta, peas, lentils, and barley are tender. Makes 12 servings.

Tortellini Soup Mix

Layer ingredients in quart jar or Mylar bag, and seal accordingly.

1 t salt	1 T dried parsley
2 T dried Italian	1 T dried minced garlic
seasoning	3-1/2 c dried tortellini pasta
4 T chicken bouillon	
granules	

Add In: 1 can kidney beans
1 can chicken (5 oz.) or 1 c cooked chicken
3 cans diced tomatoes (14 oz. each), un-drained

Directions: In a large stock pot, boil 12-16 cups water and contents of jar or bag. Cook on high until tortellini is tender. Reduce heat and add beans, tomatoes, and chicken. Simmer until heated through. Serve with warm bread.

Mediterranean Bean Soup Mix

Place beans in quart jar or Mylar bag. Combine spices in a baggy, and place the baggy in the jar or Mylar bag with beans. Seal accordingly.

3-1/2 c large white beans
(such as Cannellini or Great Northern)

Spice Baggy:

2 t dried rosemary   2 T dried celery
2 T dried minced garlic   1 T dried minced onion
2 T dried parsley flakes

Add-In: 1 can diced tomatoes (14 oz.), un-drained
1/2 lb. uncooked sausage (recommended), or 1 can chicken or ham
Salt and pepper to taste

Directions: In a large stock pot, cover beans with 16 cups water and soak overnight. Drain and rinse the beans. In the same pot, combine beans and 16 cups cold water. Bring to boil. Reduce heat and simmer 1 hour. Add contents of spice baggy, tomatoes, and meat. Simmer 35-45 minutes. If using whole sausages, remove from pot, chop into bite-size pieces, and return to pot. Add salt and pepper to taste. Makes 16 cups.

Dinners
And
Side Dishes

Chicken Fettuccine Alfredo

Combine sauce ingredients in a baggy. Place fettuccine and baggy in quart jar or Mylar bag, and seal accordingly.

1 lb. fettuccine, broken in half

Sauce Baggy:

1/4 c flour	1 c dried powdered milk
2 t salt	1/2 t black pepper
1 t parsley	pinch nutmeg

Add-In: 1 t butter
1 small can of mushrooms (optional)
1 large can of chicken*
3/4 c grated Parmesan cheese

Directions: In a large saucepan, melt butter over medium heat. Add 3 cups water. Whisk in contents of baggy and bring to a boil. Add the mushrooms (if using) and chicken. Reduce heat and simmer for 5 to 10 minutes. In a large pot, boil about 4 quarts of water. Add pasta and cook until tender, about 10-12 minutes. Drain pasta. Mix sauce with pasta and serve. Servings 4-6

Beef Stroganoff

Place noodles in a wide-mouthed quart jar or Mylar bag. You may have to break some noodles and shake them down. Add the remaining ingredients, and seal accordingly.

3 c uncooked egg noodles	1/8 t dried thyme
1/4 c nonfat dry milk	1/8 t black pepper
2 T cornstarch	1 t dried parsley
1 t onion flakes	1/2 t garlic powder
2-1/2 t beef bouillon granules	1/8 t dried basil

(continued next page)

Add-In: 1 lb. ground beef, cooked and drained
1/2 c sour cream
2 c water
1 can of mushrooms (optional)

Directions: Combine all ingredients except sour cream. Simmer 20 minutes or until noodles are tender. Stir in sour cream and serve. Servings 4-6

Spaghetti Dinner

Combine spice ingredients in a baggy. Place spaghetti and baggy in quart jar or in Mylar bag, and seal accordingly.

1 lb. spaghetti (broken in half)

Spice Baggy:

1 T instant minced onion   1 t oregano
1 t instant minced garlic   1 t Italian seasoning
2 t dried basil flakes   1 T cornstarch
1 T parsley flakes   1-1/2 t salt

Add-In: 1/2 to 1 lb. ground beef
1 can tomato paste (6 oz.)
1 can tomato sauce (15 oz.)
2 T Parmesan cheese

Directions: Brown beef in skillet; drain. Add contents of baggy, tomato paste, tomato sauce, and 2 cups water. Simmer for about 20-30 minutes, stirring occasionally. Meanwhile, cook pasta in boiling water until tender, and drain. Top pasta with meat sauce. Sprinkle with additional cheese. Servings 4-6

Skillet Tuna Casserole

Place all ingredients in a quart jar or Mylar bag. Tap jar or bag gently on countertop to shake ingredients down, and seal accordingly.

3 c egg noodles (8 oz.)   1/2 t dried parsley flakes
1 c dry milk powder   1/2 t dried chives
1/2 t dried basil   1/2 t dried oregano
1-1/2 t vegetable bouillon
granules

Add-In: 1 can cream of mushroom soup (10-3/4 oz.)
1 or 2 cans tuna, drained
1 can peas, drained (may use frozen peas)
1/4 c Parmesan cheese

Directions: In a large skillet, whisk together 3 cups of water, contents of jar or bag, and cream of mushroom soup. Bring to boil. Reduce heat and simmer for 10 minutes, stirring frequently. Add tuna and peas. Simmer 5 to 10 minutes longer until thickened. Servings 4-6

Skillet Chicken Noodle Casserole

Place all ingredients in a quart jar or Mylar bag. Tap jar or bag gently on countertop to shake ingredients down, and seal accordingly.

3 c egg noodles (8 oz.)   1/2 t dried chives
1/2 t dried parsley flakes   1 c dry milk powder
1 t Italian seasoning   1-1/2 t chicken bouillon
                                 granules

(continued next page)

117

Add-In: 1 can cream of mushroom soup (10 3/4 oz.)
1 or 2 small cans chicken (12 oz. each), un-drained, or
1-2 cups cooked and shredded chicken
1 can mixed peas & carrots, drained.)
1/4 c dried Parmesan cheese

Directions: In a large skillet, whisk together 3 cups of water, contents of jar or bag, and cream of mushroom soup. Bring to boil. Reduce heat and simmer for 10 minutes, stirring frequently. Add chicken and mixed vegetables. Simmer 5 to 10 minutes longer until thickened. Servings 4-6

Chicken Rice Casserole

Place all ingredients in a pint jar or small Mylar bag, starting with rice. Tap jar or bag on countertop to shake ingredients down, and seal accordingly.

2 c long grain white rice	1/2 t paprika
1 t dried minced onion	1/2 t chili powder
1 T dried celery flakes	1/2 t oregano
1 t dried parsley	1/2 t thyme
1 t garlic powder	1-1/2 T chicken bouillon
1 t Italian seasoning	granules

Add-In: 3 T olive oil or vegetable oil
1 can of chicken (12 oz.), or 1 cup cooked and shredded chicken
1 can green beans, drained

Directions: In a large skillet, combine contents of jar or bag, 4 cups of water, and oil. Bring to boil. Reduce heat and simmer for 20-30 minutes until rice is tender. Stir in chicken and green beans. Servings 4

Skillet Lasagna

In a quart jar or Mylar bag, layer all ingredients in the order listed. Tap the jar or bag gently on countertop to shake the ingredients down, and seal accordingly.

3 c egg noodles
1/4 c powdered milk
2 T cornstarch
2 T beef bouillon granules
1/4 t dried basil
1/4 t dried thyme

1/4 t black pepper
1 t dried parsley flakes
1/2 t garlic powder
1 t dried minced onion
1/4 c Parmesan cheese

Add-In: 1/2 -1 lb. ground beef
1 can tomato sauce (15 oz.)
Mozzarella cheese (optional)

Directions: Brown and drain ground beef. Add 3 cups water and bring to boil. Add tomato sauce and contents of jar or bag. Stir well to combine. Reduce heat and simmer for 15-30 minutes until pasta is tender and mixture is thick, stirring often. Top with mozzarella cheese if desired. Servings 4-6

Goulash Dinner

In a quart jar or Mylar bag, layer all ingredients in the order listed, and seal accordingly.

3 c elbow macaroni
1-1/2 t seasoning salt
1/2 t dried thyme
1/2 t garlic powder
1 T dried green/red
 bell pepper

1/2 c dried minced onion
1-1/2 t chili powder
1/4 t black pepper
3/4 t sugar

(continued next page)

Add-In: 1 lb. ground beef or 1 can of beef
3 cans stewed tomatoes (14.5 oz. each)

Directions: In a large skillet, brown and drain the beef. Add tomatoes and 1 cup water, and bring to boil. Reduce heat and simmer for 5 minutes. Stir in contents of jar or bag. Cover and simmer for 14 minutes. Uncover and simmer until macaroni is tender and sauce is thickened. Servings 4-6

Tomato Chili Mac

In a quart jar or Mylar bag, layer all ingredients in the order listed. Tap the jar or bag gently on countertop to shake the ingredients down, and seal accordingly.

3 c macaroni
1/2 c + 2 T dry milk
1/3 c cornstarch
1-1/2 t garlic powder
2 t dried onion
4 t beef bouillon granules

1/2 t dried thyme
1/4 t black pepper
2 t parsley flakes
1/2 t dried basil
2 T chili powder

Add-In: 1/2-1 lb. ground beef
3 cans diced tomatoes (15 oz. each)
Shredded cheese and sour cream (optional)

Directions: Brown and drain ground beef. Add 4 cups water, canned tomatoes, and contents of jar or bag. Whisk together to combine, and bring to boil. Reduce heat and simmer for 15-30 minutes until pasta is tender and mixture is thick, stirring often. Top with cheese and sour cream if desired. Servings 4-6

Beef Stroganoff Skillet (JAW)

Place noodle mix ingredients in a quart jar or Mylar bag. Place beef in a baggy, and put the baggy in the jar or bag with the noodle mix. Seal accordingly.

Noodle Mix:
2 c egg noodles
1/3 c Stroganoff Gravy Mix (recipe below)
1/2 c freeze-dried mushroom slices

Beef Baggy:
1-1/2 c freeze-dried ground beef or TVP Beef

Stroganoff Gravy Mix:
Combine all ingredients. Makes 7 portions, 1/3 cup each.

1 c flour	1 T garlic granules
1/2 c dried onion	1/2 c powdered sour cream
1 T onion powder	1/2 c powdered buttermilk
1 T dry parsley	1/2 c powdered milk
1/2 t ground nutmeg	2 t black pepper
1 t dry thyme	2 T salt

Directions: In a medium bowl, rehydrate beef in 1-1/2 cups hot water. Drain. In a large skillet, combine beef, noodle mix, and 3 cups water. Bring to boil. Reduce heat, cover, and simmer 15-20 minutes, removing lid once or twice to check progress and stir. Add more water if necessary. Serve when noodles are tender. Servings 2-4

Skillet Chicken Noodle Dinner (JAW)

Layer ingredients in a wide mouth quart jar or Mylar bag. Seal accordingly.

2 c egg noodles	1/4 c powdered butter
1/4 c freeze-dried peas	1 T dehydrated onion
1/4 c freeze-dried carrots	1 t Italian seasoning
1/3 c instant dry milk	1 c freeze-dried chicken
1/2 c freeze-dried mushroom slices	1/3 c powdered cheese sauce

Directions: In a large skillet, combine contents of jar or bag with 3-1/2 cups hot water. Bring to boil. Reduce heat and simmer 10-12 minutes, stirring occasionally. Turn off heat and let stand 3-5 minutes before serving. Servings 2-4

Hawaiian Teriyaki Chicken & Rice (JAW)

Layer ingredients in a wide mouth quart jar or Mylar bag. Place rice in baggy and add to jar or bag. Seal accordingly.

1 c freeze-dried chicken	2 T corn starch
1 c freeze-dried broccoli	1 t garlic granules
1/4 c dehydrated onion	1 t dried cilantro
3/4 c freeze-dried red & green bell pepper	1 pkg. NOH Hawaii Teri-burger meatloaf (1-1/2 oz.)*

*Available at most Asian markets.

Rice Baggy:
1 c long grain rice

(continued next page)

Directions: In a medium saucepan, combine rice and 2 cups boiling water. Cover and bring to boil. Reduce heat and simmer 20 minutes. Meanwhile, in a large pan, combine the meat and veggie mixture with 3-1/2 cups very hot water. Let stand 10 minutes to absorb water. Turn on heat to medium-high and cook 5-7 minutes until sauce is slightly thickened. Spoon meat and veggie mixture over rice to serve. Servings 2-4

Three Different Meals with One Base

Use the Noodle Base recipe for three different vegetarian meals! Simply change the sauce ingredients, and *voilà!*

To prepare your meals for storage, place the Noodle Base ingredients in a quart jar or Mylar bag, and then add the meal ingredients to the same jar or bag. Shake down the contents, and seal accordingly.

You can add freeze-dried meats if desired. Just store the ingredients in a Mylar bag instead of a jar for adequate space, and prepare the meal with an additional 1-1/2 cups water for each 1/2 cup meat.

Main Base

4 oz. spaghetti noodles*	1/4 c dehydrated carrot
1/2 c freeze dried peas	2 T dried onion flakes
3/4 c freeze dried zucchini	1/2 t dried basil leaves
1 c dried mushrooms	1/4 t hot pepper flakes
1/4 c freeze dried bell pepper	

*You can substitute any noodles of choice. Rice noodles are a good gluten-free option.

(continued next page)

Asian Noodle Dish (JAW)

1/4 c corn starch
1/8 c dried soy sauce
1 T vegetarian bouillon
  granules

1 t dried ground ginger
1 T garlic powder
2 T sugar

Directions: In a large pot, boil 4-1/2 cups water. Add contents of jar or bag and stir. Boil 8-10 minutes until noodles are tender. Cool 5 minutes. The sauce will thicken slightly. Serve hot.

Creamy Pasta Primavera (JAW)

1/4 c corn starch
1/4 c instant powdered milk
1 T vegetable bouillon
  granules

1 T Italian seasoning
1/2 t dried basil leaves
1/4 c sour cream
  powder

Directions: In a large pot, boil 4-1/2 cups water. Add contents of jar or bag and stir. Boil 8-10 minutes until noodles are tender. Serve hot.

Italian Pasta & Veggies (JAW)

2/3 c tomato powder
1 T Italian seasoning

1 T sugar

Directions: In a large pot, boil 5 cups water. Add contents of jar or bag and stir. Boil 8-10 minutes until noodles are tender. Serve hot.

124

Beef & Garlic Mashed Potatoes & Gravy (JAW)

Combine gravy ingredients and place in quart jar or Mylar bag. Combine the mashed potato ingredients in a baggy, and place the baggy in the jar or Mylar bag. Seal accordingly.

Gravy:

2 c freeze-dried diced beef
1/3 c dehydrated onion
2 t beef bouillon granules
1 t seasoning salt
1/4 c freeze-dried mushrooms

1/4 c cornstarch
1 t dried minced garlic
1 T tomato powder

Mashed Potato Baggy:

1-1/2 c potato flakes/pearls
1 t granulated garlic

1 t dried chives
3 T powdered butter

Directions: Carefully remove mashed potato baggy from jar or Mylar bag and set aside. In a medium pot, combine 4 cups very hot water with gravy mixture. Whisk well and simmer for 15-20 minutes. Turn off heat and leave covered for 5 minutes. Meanwhile, in a separate pot, boil 3 cups water. Add contents of mashed potato baggy and stir well. Let the potato mixture sit for 3-5 minutes. Fluff potatoes with a fork. Spoon gravy over potatoes to serve.

Broccoli Chicken Rice Casserole (JAW)

Place rice in quart jar or Mylar bag. Combine sauce ingredients in a baggy, and place the baggy in the jar or Mylar bag. Seal accordingly.

2 c white grain rice

(continued next page)

Sauce Baggy:

1/4 c freeze-dried celery
1/4 c dehydrated onion
1 c freeze-dried broccoli
1/2 c freeze-dried chicken

1 t seasoning salt
1/2 c powdered cheese sauce
1/4 c powdered butter

Directions: In a medium pot, combine rice and 4 cups water. Bring to boil. Reduce heat, cover, and simmer for 20-25 minutes until rice is tender. Meanwhile, in a saucepan, combine 3-1/2 cups water (2 cups water if you omit freeze-dried chicken) and contents of sauce baggy. Bring to a boil. Reduce heat and simmer 5-6 minutes. Turn off heat and let stand 5-6 minutes. Serve broccoli-cheese sauce over rice.

Scalloped Potatoes & Ham Au Gratin (JAW)

Place all ingredients in quart jar or Mylar bag. Shake down ingredients and seal accordingly.

1/2 c freeze dried ham (optional)
1/2 c dried bell peppers
1 t seasoning salt
2 T dehydrated celery slices
1/4 c powdered cheese sauce

2 T dehydrated onion
2/3 c all purpose flour*
1/2 c dry powdered milk
2 T butter powder
2-1/2 c dehydrated potato slices

*You may substitute corn starch for flour.

Directions: In a deep skillet, boil 6 cups water (4-1/2 cups water if you omit freeze-dried ham). Add contents of jar or

(continued next page)

or Mylar bag, and return to a slow boil over medium heat. Once boiling, reduce heat to very low and cook for 15 minutes, uncovered, stirring often. Turn off heat. Cover pan and let stand for 10-15 minutes until potatoes and ham are completely soft.

Pizza Mix

Combine flour, baking powder, and salt. Place in quart jar or Mylar bag. In a small baggy, combine sauce seasoning ingredients, and place baggy inside jar or Mylar bag. Seal accordingly.

2-1/2 c bread flour   2 t salt
2-3/4 t baking powder OR1-1/3 t baking soda (if using baking soda, omit salt)

Sauce Seasoning Baggy:

1 t dried garlic granules	1/4 t dried marjoram
3/4 t minced onion flakes	1/4 t dried basil
1/4 t dried oregano	1/8 t dried red pepper flakes

Sauce Add-In: 1 can tomato paste (6 oz.)
3 T Parmesan cheese

Dough Add-In: 2 T olive oil

Other Add-In: Your favorite pizza toppings

Directions:

For sauce, combine tomato paste, Parmesan cheese, 3/4 cup warm water, and contents of sauce seasoning baggy. Let set for 20-30 minutes to blend flavors.

(continued next page)

For dough, pour 3/4 -1 cup warm water into a large bowl. Add olive oil and contents of jar or bag. Stir until the dough forms a ball. If dough is very stiff, add more water. It should be soft, not sticky. Knead on a floured surface for 3-4 minutes. Roll out on baking sheet.

Top dough with sauce and your favorite toppings. Bake at 400°F for 15-25 minutes.

Side Dishes

Herb Rice Mix

Combine all ingredients. Place in pint jar or Mylar bag, and seal accordingly.

1 t dried marjoram	1/4 t dried basil
1 t dried thyme	2 t salt
1 t dried rosemary	2 c uncooked long-grain
4 t chicken bouillon	white rice
granules	

Add In: 1/4 c olive oil or butter

Directions: In a large saucepan, combine contents of jar or bag with oil and 4 cups water. Bring to boil. Reduce heat to low. Cover and cook 15 minutes or until rice is tender and liquid is absorbed. Fluff with a fork. Makes 6-8 servings.

Curried Rice

Combine all ingredients. Place in pint jar or Mylar bag, and seal accordingly.

2 T dried onion flakes
1/2 t garlic powder
1/2 t curry powder
1-1/2 c uncooked long-grain rice

1/2 c raisins
1/2 t salt
1 T chicken bouillon granules

Add-In: 1/4 cup butter or olive oil

Directions: In a large saucepan, boil 3 cups water. Add contents of jar or bag, and butter/oil. Reduce heat to low. Cover and simmer for 20-30 minutes until rice is tender and liquid is absorbed. Makes 4-6 servings.

Veggie Rice Mix (JAW)

Combine all ingredients. Place in pint jar or Mylar bag, and seal accordingly.

2 t dried celery flakes
1 t dried butter
1 t seasoning salt
1 T vegetable or chicken bouillon granules

2 t dried onion flakes
4 t dried green or red bell pepper flakes
2 c uncooked long-grain rice

Directions: In a large saucepan, combine contents of jar or bag with 4 cups water. Bring to boil. Reduce heat to low. Cover and cook 15-25 minutes, until liquid is absorbed and rice is tender. Great with any meat, poultry, or fish. Makes 6-8 servings.

Spanish Rice Mix

Combine all ingredients. Place in pint jar or Mylar bag, and seal accordingly.

1 t dried oregano	1 t dried garlic granules
1 t chili powder	1-1/2 t cumin
1 T dried chives	1-3/4 c uncooked
1 T beef or chicken bouillon granules	long-grain rice

Add-In: 1 can stewed tomatoes
1 T olive oil

Directions: In a large saucepan or skillet, combine contents of jar or bag with oil, tomatoes (un-drained), and 4-1/2 cups water. Bring to boil. Reduce heat to low. Cover and simmer 15-25 minutes, stirring often, until liquid is absorbed and rice is tender. Makes 6-8 servings.

Instant Mashed Potato Packets (JAW)

Cut gallon size Mylar bag in half make sure three sides are sealed. Place ingredients in Mylar Bag, label and seal accordingly.

2 c potato flakes	3 T butter powder
1/3 c powdered milk	1/2 t salt
2 t. dried chives	

Garlic Flavor Add: 2 1/2 t garlic granules to packet
Cheese Flavor Add: 3 T powder cheese to packet

Directions: Bring 3 cups of water to a boil. Remove from heat, stir in potato packet and let stand until moist. Whip lightly with fork and serve. Serves 6

Ramen Noodles (Individual Packets) (JAW)

Cut gallon size Mylar bags into fours. Seal three edges, fill and seal accordingly.

You can purchase plain ramen type noodles from your local Asian market, they come plain in a package of 10 or 12 in a pack and are very inexpensive.

1 cake of ramen noodle
2 T dried peas
1 T dried corn
1/4 t red or/and green
bell pepper flakes

1/8 t dried onion flakes
1 1/2 t chicken bouillon
dash garlic granules

Place ramen noodle in bag and then add remaining ingredients.

Directions: Open ramen noodle packet and place in soup bowl, add 1to 1 1/4 cup of boiled water cove with small plate and wait 12 minutes and eat.

Treats
And
Sweets

M&M Cookie Mix (NRLT)

Layer ingredients in quart jar or Mylar bag in the order listed, and seal accordingly.

2 c all-purpose flour   3/4 c brown sugar, packed
1/2 t baking soda   1/4 c sugar
1/4 t baking powder   1-1/4 c M&M's

Add-In: 1/2 c butter, softened
1 egg, beaten
1 t vanilla*

Directions: Empty contents of jar or bag into mixing bowl and stir to combine. Add butter, egg, and vanilla. Mix until completely blended. Roll into 1-inch balls. Place balls 2 inches apart on ungreased cookie sheet. Bake at 375° until edges are lightly browned, about 12 to 14 minutes.

S'mores Delight (NRLT)

Combine crushed graham crackers and powdered buttermilk, and place in quart jar or Mylar bag. Layer remaining ingredients over graham cracker mixture, ending with marshmallows. If using a jar, press the marshmallows down firmly over other ingredients. Seal accordingly.

1-1/2 c graham crackers   1-1/2 T powered buttermilk
(crushed)   4 c dried coconut flakes
3/4 c chocolate pieces   2 c mini marshmallows
or M&M's

Add-In: 1/2 c butter, melted
1 t vanilla*

(continued next page)

Directions: In a large mixing bowl, thoroughly mix contents of jar or bag with melted butter, vanilla, and 1/3 cup water. Press lightly into greased 9 x 9 inch pan. Bake at 350° for 15 minutes. Cool completely before cutting.

Choc O' Nut Cookie Mix (NRLT)

Layer all ingredients in quart jar or Mylar bag, and seal accordingly.

1-1/3 c all-purpose flour
1/4 t baking soda
1/8 t salt
2/3 c packed brown sugar
1/2 c honey-roasted peanuts or chopped pecans

3/4 c M&M's or chocolate pieces
1/2 c flaked coconut

Add-In: 1/2 cup butter, softened
1 egg
1 t vanilla*

Directions: In a large mixing bowl, beat butter with an electric mixer on medium to high speed until smooth. Beat in egg and vanilla until well combined. With a wooden spoon, stir in contents of jar or bag until well combined. Drop by tablespoons onto ungreased cookie sheets. Lightly press down to flatten. Bake at 350° for 12 minutes or until edges are lightly browned.

* To include the vanilla with your pre-assembled mix instead adding at preparation, stir the vanilla into the white sugar and allow to air dry. Then add the vanilla-sugar to your jar or Mylar bag.

Sugar Cookies

Combine flour, baking powder, baking soda, and salt. Pour sugar into bottom of jar or Mylar bag. Top with flour mixture. Label and seal accordingly.

3 c all-purpose flour	1/8 t salt
1 t baking powder	1-1/2 c white sugar
1 t baking soda	

Add-In: 1 c butter, softened
2 eggs
1/2 t lemon extract
1 t vanilla extract*
Decorating sugar or icing (optional)

Directions: Empty contents of jar or bag into large mixing bowl. Cut in butter until the mixture is crumbly. In a separate bowl, beat eggs, vanilla, and lemon extract until light and fluffy. Add egg mixture to dry ingredients and mix until well blended. Cover bowl and chill 1 hour. Preheat oven to 350°. On a lightly floured surface, roll dough to 1/4-inch thickness. Cut into desired shapes with cookie cutters. Place cookies 1-1/2 inches apart on cookie sheets. Sprinkle with decorating sugar if desired. Bake 10 to 12 minutes in preheated oven until edges begin to brown. Cool completely. When cool, decorate un-sugared cookies with icing if desired.

Kettle Chip Cookies (NRLT)

Combine flour and baking powder and place in bottom of a wide-mouthed quart jar or Mylar bag. Layer remaining ingredients on top of flour mixture. If using jar, press each layer down firmly before adding the next ingredient. Label and seal accordingly.

(continued next page)

2-1/2 c all-purpose flour   1-1/2 c crushed potato
1 c white sugar   chips
1 t baking powder   2/3 c chopped pecans

Add-In: 2 sticks butter, softened
1 t vanilla

Directions: Preheat oven to 350°. Empty contents of jar or bag into large mixing bowl, and stir to combine ingredients. Add butter and vanilla. Mix well. Shape into 1-inch balls and place 1-1/2 inches apart on ungreased cookie sheet. Flatten slightly. Bake in preheated oven for 14-18 minutes until edges are very lightly browned. Cool 5 minutes on cookie sheets, then transfer to cooling rack to cool completely. Makes 2-1/2 dozen cookies.

Brownie Mix

Combine flour, baking powder, and salt, and set aside. Layer remaining ingredients in the order listed in quart jar or Mylar bag, finishing with flour mixture (If using jar, tap on counter between layers to settle ingredients. For a gift jar, wipe the inside with a dry paper towel after settling the cocoa to clear the glass.) Seal accordingly.

2-1/4 c white sugar   1 t baking powder
2/3 c cocoa   1 t salt
1-1/4 c all-purpose flour

Add-In: 3/4 c butter or margarine, melted
4 eggs, slightly beaten

Directions: Preheat over 350°. Empty contents of jar or

(continued next page)

bag into large mixing bowl, and stir to combine ingredients. Add butter and eggs, and mix until completely blended. Spread batter into greased 9 x 13 inch baking pan. Bake in preheated oven for 30 minutes. Cool completely. Cut into small squares. Makes 2 dozen.

Butterscotch Cookie Mix (NRLT)

Combine flour, baking powder, and baking soda. Place flour mixture in bottom of quart jar or Mylar bag. Layer all remaining ingredients over the flour mixture. If using jar, tap on counter to settle ingredients. Seal accordingly.

Note: This cookie mix is not recommended for long term storage because of the fat in the butterscotch chips and the moisture in the brown sugar. If you want to prepare the mix for long-term storage, simply omit the chips and brown sugar, and include them as add-ins at preparation.

1-1/2 c all-purpose flour	1/2 c crispy rice cereal
3/4 t baking soda	1/4 c white sugar
1/4 t baking powder	3/4 c packed brown sugar
1 c butterscotch chips	1/2 c rolled oats

Add-In: 1/2 c butter or margarine
3 to 4 T water
1 egg, slightly beaten*

Directions: Preheat oven to 350°. In large mixing bowl, cream butter, egg, and 3 to 4 tablespoons water. Add contents of jar or bag and mix until well combined. Drop dough by tablespoon onto an ungreased cookie sheet. Bake in preheated oven for 12 minutes.

*Can use 4 teaspoons of dried egg whites instead of fresh eggs.

Vanilla Pudding Mix (Bulk Recipe) (JAW)

Combine all ingredients well. Divide into any size jars or Mylar bags. Seal accordingly.

7 c nonfat dry milk   1 t salt
5 c vanilla sugar*   3 c cornstarch
1/2 t nutmeg

Directions: Combine 3/4 cup of mix with 2 cups water in a medium sauce pan. Heat and stir constantly while simmering until thickened. Cool completely.

* To make vanilla sugar, stir 3 tablespoons vanilla extract into 5 cups white sugar and allow to air dry. Stir while drying. When dry, break up into granules again, stir in remaining sugar for the recipe.

Chocolate Pudding Mix (Bulk Recipe) (JAW)

Combine all ingredients well. Divide into any size jars or Mylar bags. Seal accordingly.

5 c sugar   2-1/2 t salt
3 c cornstarch   3-1/3 c unsweetened
7 c instant nonfat   cocoa
dry milk

Directions: Shake bag or jar to combine ingredients well. In medium saucepan, combine 3/4 cup mix with 2 cups water. Cook over low heat, stirring constantly until mixture comes to a boil. Continue to cook and stir one minute longer. Remove from heat. Pour into serving bowl and let cool.

Index

Dinners

Dip Mixes

Treats and Sweets

For more copies contact:
Janice Paveglio Gunther
e-mail guntherjk@gmail.com

Or visit us for more information and products at:
www.prepnstore.com